Principles of
MARKETING

CLEP* Test Study Guide

All rights reserved. This Study Guide, Book and Flashcards are protected under the US Copyright Law. No part of this book or study guide or flashcards may be reproduced, distributed or stored in a retrieval system, or transmitted in any form or by any means, electronic, mechanical, photocopying, recording, or otherwise, without the prior written permission of the publisher Breely Crush Publishing, LLC.

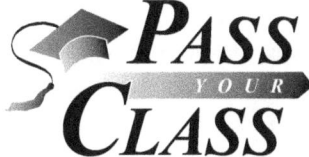

© 2026 Breely Crush Publishing, LLC

*CLEP is a registered trademark of the College Entrance Examination Board which does not endorse this book.

971052024143

Copyright ©2003 - 2026, Breely Crush Publishing, LLC.

All rights reserved.

This Study Guide, Book and Flashcards are protected under the US Copyright Law. No part of this publication may be reproduced, distributed or stored in a retrieval system, or transmitted in any form or by any means, electronic, mechanical, photocopying, recording, or otherwise, without the prior written permission of the publisher Breely Crush Publishing, LLC.

Published by Breely Crush Publishing, LLC
10808 River Front Parkway
South Jordan, UT 84095
www.breelycrushpublishing.com

ISBN-13: 978-1-61433-648-8

Printed and bound in the United States of America.

*CLEP is a registered trademark of the College Entrance Examination Board which does not endorse this book.

Table of Contents

The Marketing Concepts – An Overview *1*
   What is Marketing? *1*
   Marketing System *3*
The Marketing Opportunities – An Analysis *5*
   the Marketing Environment *5*
   Consumer Market and an Analysis of Buyer Behavior *7*
   Organizational, Reseller and Government Markets *20*
Organizing for Marketing Efforts *22*
   Basic Objectives and Strategies *22*
   Marketing Organization *26*
   Types of Planning in Marketing *28*
Planning and Marketing Mix *30*
   Types of Products and Product Traits *30*
   The Product Mix Decisions *31*
   Channels of Distribution *34*
   Product Promotion Efforts *40*
   Advertising *43*
   Price Determination *43*
   Marketing Effort Control *47*
The Seven Steps of Selling *48*
Writing a Marketing Plan *49*
Legal Aspects of Marketing *50*
   Legislation *50*
   Taxes *51*
Online Marketing *51*
   Banner Ads *51*
   Cost Per Click (CPC) *51*
   Impressions *52*
   Conversions *52*
   Remarketing *52*
   Click-through rate (CTR) *52*
   Search Engine Marketing (SEM) *54*
   Social Media Marketing *54*
   Content Marketing *54*
   Email Marketing *55*
   Affiliate Marketing *55*
   Video Marketing *55*
Sample Test Questions *57*
Test Taking Strategies *96*

What Your Score Means *97*
Test Preparation *97*
Legal Note *98*
References *98*

The Marketing Concepts – An Overview

WHAT IS MARKETING?

In layman's language, a "market" generally means a place where sellers and buyers meet to exchange what they have in excess for what they require. Sellers sell products for money, and buyers buy products in exchange for their money.

Marketing is highly influenced by change. Change in any area of a buyer's life can influence the way they spend money. Some types of changes that have to be taken into consideration are social, economic, technological, political, and legal changes.

Social changes are changes which relate to behavior and lifestyle. For example, changes in fashion are considered social changes. Another factor to consider would be the age structure of a population. Analyzing these factors (and changes in them) can give a company a sense of what the market will be like in the future.

Changes in the economy also have a large effect on buying patterns. In a bad economy, people are less likely to spend money, and most businesses suffer. On the other hand, when the economy is doing well, all businesses benefit. Changes in inflation, interest rates, and average wages are also economic changes.

Technological changes are also important. Increased internet usage affects marketing strategy, advancements in consumer technology create new and ever changing products and new production technology allows products to be made and shipped faster and cheaper. Technology affects all levels of marketing. This makes keeping up with the changes an important element of marketing.

Political changes can affect international trade. For example, the creation of the European Union opened up trade among all European nations. For the United States, politics relating to Middle Eastern countries has a significant effect on gas prices.

Legal changes also have the potential to affect marketing. In the early 1900s, the antitrust movement completely changed the way businesses operated. Today, laws regarding environmental issues, consumer protection, labor, and other factors regulate how businesses are allowed to market and function.

Marketing: This can be defined as a set of activities undertaken by human beings aimed at promoting and completing exchanges.

Marketing Management – A Definition: The core concept behind marketing has to do with exchange. Marketing Management, therefore, is the analysis, ideation, planning, organizing, executing and controlling of stated targets with pre-identified audiences for mutual gain. To get an effective response, an Optimal Marketing Decision Variables is arrived at, which works as a blueprint for success.

SALES AND MARKETING CONCEPTS:

SALES: aims to achieve:

| Increased Sales Volumes and Good Profits | through | Hard Sell and Promotion | of | PRODUCTS |

MARKETING: aims to achieve:

| Profits through Customer Satisfaction | through | Integrated Marketing | of | What the Customer wants |

An Integrated Marketing Approach always works in terms of the customer's needs, desires and wants and places them above company needs. Let us see where a Marketing Department lies in an organizational setup and with what authority structures.

MARKETING SYSTEM

In a basic model, a company dispatches goods and services to the market, together with communication, and in exchange, receives money value (Dollars) for the goods plus information. But today's marketing system has become more complex and sophisticated. Today's marketing system is given in a schematic diagram for easy understanding:

INNER CORE

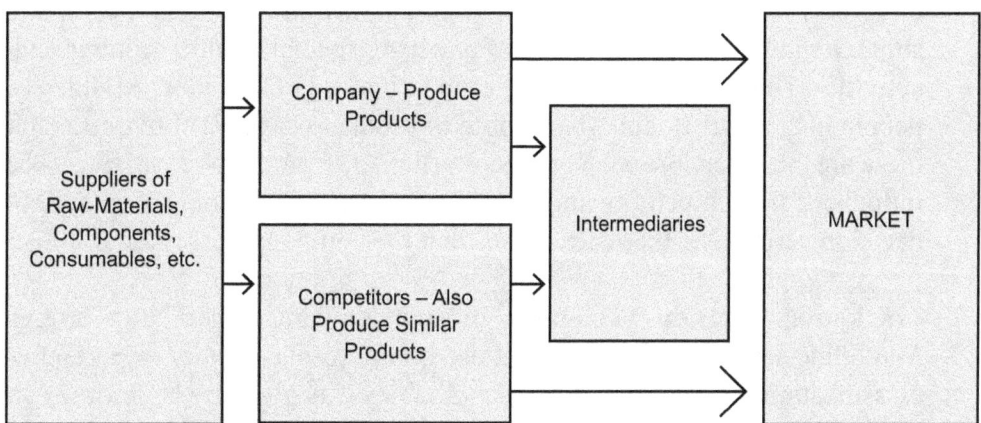

This is the inner core of today's marketing system. This, of course, is enveloped by an outer core, which is as important as the inner core.

OUTER CORE

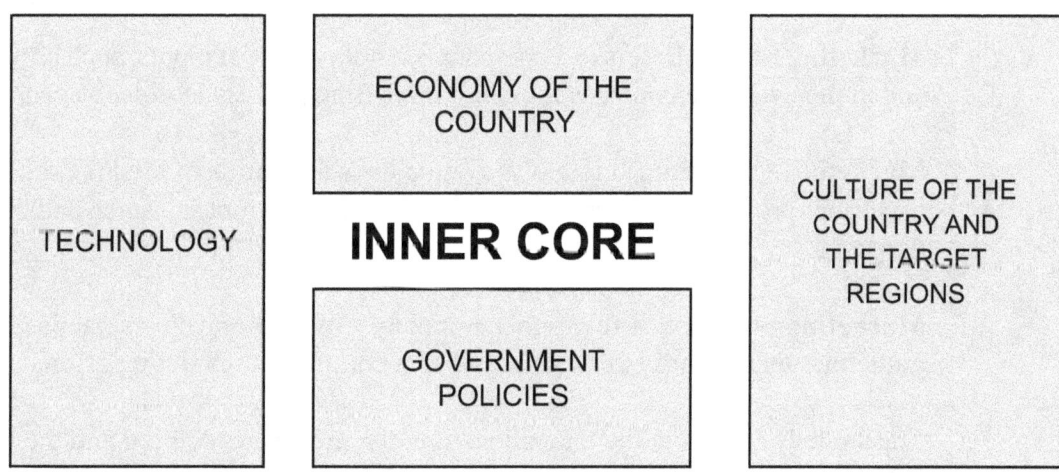

If technology is fast changing, the marketing effort will be affected. Likewise, if the economy is bad, it may tell upon marketing your product. Government policies have a major say in your marketing. Good business-friendly policies will encourage you into putting more effort in marketing. The culture of the country, as well as the region where your target market is situated, will also have a role to play. In the USA, beef eating is common and plenty of beef is consumed daily. But in India, where the Hindu culture demands abstinence from consuming beef, marketing beef products would take a unique approach.

Demand Variables: These are causes that have the potential to negatively affect the sales of a company or the entire industry. Example: A car company's sales are affected by the people's attitude towards cars, disposable income, infrastructure facilities and the general conditions of roads, the cost of petrol/diesel as the case may be, the total of high as well as upper middle class groups within the country, competitors and their strategies in terms of price, terms of payment, special product features and promotional activities. Demand variables are grouped into: (1) Customer variables (a) number of people in the market, and, (b) the rate of product usage. (2) Environmental variables – these are the outer core we have seen earlier. (3) Competitive variables – causes that are influenced by competitors and have a role in affecting your sales, and, (4) Marketing decision variables – these are causes that the company possesses to influence sales.

Marketing Decision Variables: In any company's marketing program, it is the Marketing Decision Variables that are bound to play a very important role. The best classification of marketing decision variables was given by E. Jerome McCarthy – the "Four P's" – (1) Product (2) Place (3) Promotion and (4) Price.

Marketing Mix: It is the most important task of the Marketing Department to find out the optimum setting for its Marketing Decision Variables. This Optimum Setting is considered the Marketing Mix of the company.

Marketing Effort: Refers to a company's employment of inputs, such as men, material and money, into the company's overall marketing process in order to generate sales.

Marketing Allocation: It refers to a company's allocation of total marketing efforts to its various products, different customer segments, different salesmen and different sales divisions.

Marketing Strategy: It refers to a company's overall objectives, tactics, policies and guidelines that govern over a period of that company's marketing effort.

The strategy spells out the total allocation, the ideal mix required and the level of marketing efforts needed to achieve a predetermined target. Environmental changes and the level of competitive thrust determine the overall strategy.

Market Response: It relates to the response in the pattern of sales to the marketing effort.

The Marketing Opportunities – An Analysis

THE MARKETING ENVIRONMENT

An organization dealing in the marketing of products works in a complicated and fast changing marketing environment. Constant vigil to identify impending changes and swift adaptation to such changes allows an organization to survive and better still, prosper. A marketing environment consists of a number of tiers. They are: (1) the organization of a corporate environment, (2) the market environment, and (3) the macro environment. An organization and its Macro Environment together form an Ecosystem. Turbulence in the ecosystem either creates threats or opportunities to organizations depending upon their attitude.

THE TIERS OF A PRODUCTS MARKETING ENVIRONMENT

The marketing macro-environment is very important, and therefore, let us study the four factors of which it is composed. The economic environment symbolizes the rising income of persons, and as a corollary, the changing patterns of retailing, wholesaling and physical distribution. The technological factor indicates the speed with which products become obsolete on account of technological innovations, and increased R&D expenses on account of the company's quest to find a more stable product. The Government policy factor compels you to constantly and consistently look for policy changes and adapt to new policies. The culture factor ensures safe life and that long perceived and followed beliefs are not impaired. Of these four factors, let us study in detail the Economy factor, which is vital for many decisions a company has to make as it impacts the market. Cyclical changes in the economy's overall level of business are known as the business cycle. There are four stages in any business cycle:

(1) Prosperity (also known as boom)

(2) Recession (it is a slowdown of business)

(3) Depression (gloom, also called bust stage)

(4) Recovery (the economic upswing)

Why do swings take place? It is because of variations in the demand and supply continuum for goods, the volume of consumer spending, level of employment, the consumers' ability (that is, level of disposable income), interest rates, Government Tax policy and spending. If there is a huge demand, the business invests in more machinery and plants to meet such increases.

Inflation: This refers to a decline in purchasing power due to price levels rising faster than income. This can happen at any stage of the business cycle.

THE COMPETITIVE ENVIRONMENT AND THE MARKET STRUCTURE

All producers and marketing organizations vie for the general customers' purchasing power. The competitive environment is governed by the market structure within which it operates. In market structure there are four basic types:

1. Pure Competition – many small sellers and many small buyers; none of them individually can affect any changes on demand and supply.

2. Monopolistic Competition – many sellers and many buyers, but their products have subtle or vast differentiation from the others.

3. Oligopoly – a few large sellers account for the major portion of total industry sales – Branding with unique selling propositions helps.

4. Pure Monopoly – this is just the reverse of pure competition. Large public sector units dominate the industry. Literally no competition is allowed.

CONSUMER MARKET AND AN ANALYSIS OF BUYER BEHAVIOR

Today, all markets are complex and unique. To understand the essentials of markets, a marketing system needs a general framework, which tries to understand the market's composition, character, needs and wants. There are four questions that will give an insight into this system:

1. What did the market use to buy? This gives you an insight into the <u>objects</u> of purchase.
2. Why buy? This gives an insight into the <u>objectives</u> of such purchases.
3. Who is buying? This gives an insight into the <u>organization</u> for such purchases.
4. How does it buy? This gives an insight into the general <u>working of the organization</u> that affects purchasing.

THE 4 – P'S OR THE COMPONENTS OF MARKETING DECISION VARIABLES:

According to the specific characteristics of individual markets, the 4-P's of Marketing Decision variables are set. In a market where price is most sensitive, the organization tries to maintain the existing price levels even if a price increase from the organization's point of view is justified; it may offer more liberal credit terms or allow some allowances on the basis of more off-take, etc.

Consumer markets play a crucial role in the economy. They encompass the buying and selling of goods and services for personal, non-business use. In these markets, purchases are made by individuals or households to satisfy their own needs and desires. The United States boasts one of the largest consumer markets in the world, catering to over 300 million people who collectively spend trillions of dollars on various products and services.

Marketing professionals have long recognized the diversity within consumer markets and have developed strategies to target specific groups and sub-groups based on their unique needs and preferences. By segmenting the market into categories such as men, women, children, youth, and the elderly, companies can create products and services tailored to each group's requirements. This approach allows businesses to effectively reach their target audience and maximize their market share.

To better understand the intricacies of consumer markets, it is essential to establish a classification system for the vast array of consumer products available. This classification helps marketers identify the underlying differences between product types and develop appropriate marketing mix strategies.

One fundamental distinction in product classification is between consumer and industrial products. The primary difference lies in their intended purpose and the buyer's identity. Individuals purchase consumer products for personal or household use, which are typically found in retail stores. Examples of consumer products include everyday items like groceries, clothing, electronics, and household appliances. For instance, a family might purchase a new refrigerator to replace an old one or buy a set of dishes for their home.

On the other hand, industrial products are designed to be bought by companies and used in the production of other goods or services. These products encompass raw materials, components, and machinery used in manufacturing processes. For example, a car manufacturer may purchase large quantities of steel, aluminum, and plastic to construct vehicles. Similarly, a textile company might acquire industrial sewing machines to mass-produce clothing items.

Interestingly, some products can be classified as either consumer or industrial, depending on the context and purpose of their purchase. A prime example is flour. When an individual buys a five-pound bag of flour to bake cookies at home, it is considered a consumer good. However, when a commercial bakery purchases several thousand pounds of flour to produce pastries on a large scale, the flour becomes an industrial good.

The classification of products as consumer or industrial has significant implications for marketing strategies. Consumer products often require extensive advertising and promotion to create brand awareness and drive sales. Companies may employ various marketing channels, such as television commercials, social media campaigns, and in-store displays, to reach potential customers. The focus is often on the emotional appeal and benefits of the product, as well as its price and convenience.

In contrast, marketing strategies for industrial products tend to be more targeted and relationship-oriented. Companies selling industrial goods often rely on personal selling, trade shows, and direct marketing to reach their target audience. The emphasis is on the product's technical specifications, performance, and reliability, as well as the seller's expertise and after-sales support.

Another crucial aspect of consumer markets is the influence of demographic factors on purchasing behavior. Age, gender, income level, education, and cultural background can all play a role in shaping consumer preferences and decision-making processes. For example, a luxury car manufacturer may target affluent, middle-aged professionals, while a toy company might focus on children and their parents.

Understanding these demographic factors allows marketers to develop products and promotional strategies that resonate with specific consumer segments. A skincare company, for instance, may create a line of anti-aging products specifically designed for women over 50, while a sportswear brand might develop a range of athletic clothing tailored to the needs and preferences of young, active men.

The rise of e-commerce and digital technologies has transformed the landscape of consumer markets. Online shopping platforms like Amazon and eBay have made it easier for consumers to access a wide variety of products from the comfort of their homes. Social media and mobile applications have also become powerful tools for marketers to engage with consumers, build brand loyalty, and drive sales.

Consumer markets are vast and dynamic, encompassing the diverse needs and preferences of individuals and households. By understanding the distinctions between consumer and industrial products, as well as the demographic factors that influence purchasing behavior, marketers can develop effective strategies to reach and satisfy their target audiences. As technology continues to evolve and shape consumer habits, companies must adapt their approaches to remain competitive in an ever-changing marketplace.

DURABLE GOODS – NON-DURABLE GOODS AND SERVICES

Durable Goods: These tangible goods (actual goods), once bought, will satisfy you for many years (Example: Air conditioners, refrigerators, clothing, etc.).

Non-Durable Goods: These are also tangible goods, which once bought may be consumed in a very short period of time (Example: Toothpaste, soap, ham, biscuits, etc.).

Services: These are non-tangible activities, benefits and satisfactions that are offered by individuals with expertise (Example: Tailoring, hair dressing, cleaning, general repairing, etc.).

The general characteristics in relation to marketing of durable, non-durable and services are:

Durable Goods – Needs more personal selling, more seller guarantees and to charge a higher margin.

Non-Durable Goods and Services – To develop loyalty over time, marketed in a number of locations, charging a small margin. Any marketing strategy should be tailored to meet these general characteristics.

Another classification based on consumer's purchasing habits gives us 3 different groups of goods:

1. Convenient Goods: Goods bought by consumers most often with relative speed without spending time on comparison (Example: Newspapers, soaps, detergents, tobacco products, etc.).

2. Shopping Goods: Goods bought by consumers after spending time considering its utility, value, quality, suitability, style and of course, price (Example: Cars, home appliances, dress materials, furniture, etc.).

3. Specialty Goods: Goods bought by consumers that have characteristics perceived to be unique and/or having good brand identification (Example: Branded goods, fancy goods, electronic goods, photographic equipment, etc.).

Another way that products can be classified is as heterogeneous or homogeneous. Homogeneous products are manufactured to be all the same. For example, a bread company wants all of their bread to be the same and a nail company wants every nail to be the same. In each case, if there were an inconsistent or wrong item, the company would receive complaints. However, other industries want to have diverse or varied products. In this case the products would be called heterogeneous. For example, donut shops have many different types of donuts to please as many people as possible. Another comparison would be the difference between buying a pair of jeans at the store and going to a tailor. The jeans at the store are meant to be uniform, whereas the tailor will make custom goods.

CONSUMER BEHAVIOR

What are the objectives or goals a consumer while effecting a purchase is looking for? To put it simply, he is looking for a perceived need satisfaction. Needs are unlimited.

Maslow's Hierarchy of Needs

Maslow's Hierarchy of Needs consists of the following stages from the top down:

- Self-Actualization
- Esteem Needs
- Belonging and Love
- Safety
- Physical Needs

These stages begin at the physical needs. First you need to have food, water, and shelter before you can worry about other requirements. Once those needs are met you may start to think of other necessities, such as safety. You might buy a gun or move to a more prosperous and safe area. Once you are fed, clothed and safe you will want to meet needs of belonging and love through relationships. If you feel loved, you may begin to think about your self-esteem and how you feel as a person, what you are contributing. The final stage, self-actualization, you may never meet. Most people do not.

A Buyer's buying decisions are generally influenced by the Buyer's cultural, social, personal and psychological factors. We will presently see all those factors that influence Buyer behavior.

FACTORS INFLUENCING BUYER BEHAVIOR

CULTURAL
Culture
Sub-Culture
Social Class

SOCIAL
Reference Groups
Face-to-Face Groups
Family

BUYER

PSYCHOLOGICAL
Perception
Learning
Motivation
Attitudes and Beliefs

PERSONAL
Age...
Stage in Life Cycle
Occupation
Life Style
Economic
Topography
Personality

CULTURAL FACTORS

Culture: It is the most rudimentary determinant of a person's needs and wants and the resultant behavior. As we grow, we acquire a set of values, perceptions, preferences, attitudes and behavior through social interactions. Knowledge about products and other utilities are naturally culture specific.

Sub-culture: Every culture has within itself sub-cultures. These sub-cultures provide identity to its members. Sub-cultures are grouped as:

1. Nationality Groups – Americans, Chinese, English, etc.
2. Religious Groups – Christians, Muslims, Hindus, Jews, Buddhists, etc.
3. Racial Groups – Whites, Blacks, Orientals, etc.
4. Geographical Area Groups – North American, South American, etc.

These sub-cultures condition certain cultural preferences and prohibitions fashioning clear styles and attitudes. These factors have a say in clothing preferences, food choices, career ambitions and even recreation.

Discretionary income is a crucial concept in personal finance and economics, as it represents the portion of an individual's income that remains after accounting for essential expenses and savings. This leftover money can be spent however the person chooses, giving them the financial freedom to pursue their desires and interests.

To calculate discretionary income, one must first determine their disposable income, which is the total income earned minus taxes. For instance, if an individual earns $5,000 per month and pays $1,000 in taxes, their disposable income would be $4,000. From this amount, the person must subtract their savings and cost of living expenses, such as rent or mortgage payments, groceries, utilities, and transportation costs.

Consider the following example: Sarah, a single professional, earns a monthly salary of $6,000. She pays $1,500 in taxes, setting her disposable income at $4,500. Sarah is committed to saving 10% of her disposable income each month, which amounts to $450. Her monthly expenses include $1,200 for rent, $400 for groceries, $150 for utilities, and $300 for transportation. In total, her living expenses sum up to $2,050. To calculate Sarah's discretionary income, we use the formula: discretionary income = disposable income - savings - cost of living expenses. In this case, Sarah's discretionary income equals $4,500 - $450 - $2,050, which amounts to $2,000.

The amount of discretionary income available to individuals can vary significantly based on factors such as income level, tax brackets, living expenses, and personal financial goals. Those with higher incomes and lower living costs tend to have more discretionary income, while those with lower incomes or residing in expensive areas may have limited discretionary funds.

Discretionary income not only provides individuals with the freedom to spend on non-essential items, but it also plays a vital role in driving consumer spending and economic growth. When people have more money to spend on non-essential items, such as entertainment, dining out, travel, or luxury goods, it stimulates demand for these products and services. This, in turn, benefits businesses, fosters job creation, and increases economic activity, painting a picture of a thriving economy.

For example, if a group of friends each has $500 in discretionary income per month, they may choose to spend it on a weekend getaway, dining at high-end restaurants, or purchasing the latest electronics. These expenditures contribute to the revenue of the respective businesses and support the livelihoods of those employed in these industries.

However, it is essential to note that discretionary income should not be confused with disposable income. While disposable income represents the total amount of money available after taxes, discretionary income is the portion of disposable income that remains after accounting for necessary expenses and savings. Failing to distinguish between the two can lead to financial strain if individuals overspend on non-essential items without considering their long-term financial obligations and goals.

The concept of discretionary income highlights the importance of budgeting and financial planning. By carefully tracking income, expenses, and savings, individuals can make informed decisions about how to allocate their discretionary funds. This may involve setting aside money for short-term desires while also investing in long-term goals, such as retirement or purchasing a home.

Discretionary income represents the financial freedom individuals have to spend money on non-essential items after accounting for taxes, savings, and necessary living expenses. It is a key driver of consumer spending and economic growth, but it is crucial to balance discretionary spending with long-term financial planning. By understanding and effectively managing discretionary income, individuals can enjoy the benefits of their hard-earned money while maintaining financial stability and working towards their life goals.

Social stratification is a ubiquitous phenomenon that divides individuals into hierarchical groups based on various factors, such as caste, social class, education, income, occupation, and net worth. This stratification significantly impacts the aspirations, preferences, and consumer behavior of members within each group.

A caste is a form of social stratification particularly prominent in certain societies, such as India. In a caste-based system, individuals are born into a specific caste and are expected to adhere to the traditional practices and norms associated with that caste. For example, in India, the caste system has historically determined an individual's occupation, marriage prospects, and social interactions. Members of a particular caste often have similar aspirations and follow well-defined customs and traditions.

On the other hand, social class is a more fluid form of stratification that is based on an individual's position within society. Social class is determined by a combination of factors: education, income, occupation, and net worth. Individuals within a particular social class tend to share similar values, lifestyles, and consumer preferences.

For instance, upper class members, characterized by high levels of education, income, and net worth, may prefer luxury goods and services. They may frequent exclusive restaurants, resorts, and country clubs, and may have a taste for high-end fashion, art, and collectibles. An example of this would be a CEO of a Fortune 500 company who drives a premium luxury car, owns multiple properties and takes regular vacations to exotic destinations.

In contrast, members of the middle class, who typically have moderate levels of education and income, may have different consumption patterns. They may prioritize practicality and value for money when making purchasing decisions. For example, a middle-class family may opt for a reliable, fuel-efficient car, shop at mid-range department stores, and take an annual vacation to a domestic destination.

Lower-class individuals, who often have limited education and income, may have different aspirations and consumer behaviors. They may focus on meeting basic needs and may have a preference for affordable, essential goods and services. For instance, a low-income family may rely on public transportation, shop at discount stores, and prioritize spending on necessities like food, housing, and healthcare.

Marketers must understand the unique preferences and behaviors associated with each social class to develop targeted marketing strategies. By tailoring products, services, and promotional messages to each social class's specific needs and desires, companies can more effectively reach and engage their target audience.

For example, a luxury car manufacturer may focus on targeting upper-class individuals through exclusive events, partnerships with high-end brands, and advertising in premium publications. On the other hand, a budget-friendly grocery chain may focus on attracting lower and middle-class consumers through promotional offers, value-based messaging, and strategic store locations in working-class neighborhoods.

Social stratification, whether based on caste or social class, profoundly impacts the aspirations, preferences, and consumer behavior of individuals within each group. Understanding these differences is crucial for businesses seeking to effectively market their products and services to specific segments of society. By recognizing the unique needs and desires of each social class, companies can develop targeted strategies that resonate with their target audience and drive business success.

PERCEIVED MAJOR SOCIAL CLASSES[1]

1. **Upper Uppers:** Upper uppers are the social elite who live on inherited wealth and have well-known families. They maintain more than one home and send their children to the best schools. They are in the market for jewelry, antiques, homes and foreign vacations. While small as a group, they serve as a representative group for others to the extent that their consumption decisions are imitated by other social classes. They do not believe in ostentatious or showy lifestyles.

2. **Lower Uppers:** Lower uppers are persons who have earned high income or wealth through exceptional ability in their profession or business. They usually come from the middle class. They tend to be active in social and civic affairs and seek to buy the symbols of social status for themselves and their children, such as expensive cars, homes, and schooling. They include the nouveaux riches, whose pattern of conspicuous consumption is designed to impress those below

them. Their ambition is to be accepted in the upper-upper status, a status that is more likely to be achieved by their children than themselves.

3. **Upper Middles:** Upper middles possess neither family status nor unusual wealth. They are primarily concerned with "career." They have attained positions as professionals, independent business persons, and corporate managers. They believe in education and want their children to develop professional or administration skills so that they won't drop into a lower stratum. Members of this class like to deal in ideas and "high culture." They are highly civic-minded and they are the quality marker for good clothes, homes, furniture and appliances and entertainment.

4. **Middle Class:** The middle class are average-paid white and blue collar workers who live on "the better side of town" and try to do the proper things; often they buy popular products to "keep up with the trends." The middle class believes in spending more money on "worthwhile experiences" for their children and aiming them towards professional college education. Better living means "a better home in a nice locality" with good schools.

5. **Working Class:** Working class consists of average pay blue collar workers and those who lead a "working class lifestyle," whatever income, school or job they have. The working class depends heavily on relatives for economic and emotional support, for tips on job opportunities, advice on purchase, and for assistance in times of trouble. The working class maintains sharp sex-role division and stereotyping. They tend to have larger families than the higher classes.

6. **Upper Lowers:** Upper lowers are working, although their living standard is just above poverty. They perform unskilled work and are poorly paid; often they are educationally deficient. Although they fall near the poverty line they manage to "present a picture of self-discipline" and "maintain some effort at cleanliness."

7. **Lower Lowers:** Lower lowers are visibly poverty stricken, and usually out of work. Some are not interested in finding permanent jobs and most are dependent on charity for income. Their homes, clothes and possessions are "dirty," "raggedy" and "broken-down."

SOCIAL FACTORS

Reference Groups: A person may not be a member of such groups but identifies with it and aspires to become one – such groups are known as Reference Groups. Example: A young boy adoring Michael Jordan and aspiring to become like him in Basketball, or a young girl adoring Sharon Stone and aspiring to become a star like her in Moviedom. Such persons subconsciously watch and mimic their Hero's attitudes and behavioral patterns. Such persons are influenced in the buying behavior too by their subject of adoration!

Face to Face Groups: These are groups which have direct and immediate influence on a person's opinions, likes and dislikes. Example: The person's family, friends, neighbors, peers, etc.

Family: A person's basic attitudes, behaviors and beliefs are developed during the formative years, formed through interaction with his family, which plays a most enduring role in such attitude formation. One's immediate family constitutes the most influential primary reference group. There are products with which different family members have a dominant role to play.

	Products	**Dominant Member**
1)	Television, Cell phones, Automobiles, Insurance, Air Conditioners, etc.	Husband
2)	Food items, Kitchenware, Appliances, Refrigerators, Washing Machines, etc.	Wife
3)	House, External Entertainment, Vacation and Traveling, etc.	Both Husband and Wife

Personal Factors: A person's age, state at which he is in the lifecycle, economic background, occupation, lifestyle, disposable income at his command, etc., all influence his buying behavior.

Psychological Factors: A person's needs and wants are unlimited. A specific need at a specified point of time takes precedence over others. There are (1) biogenic and (2) psychogenic needs.

The biogenic needs are concerned with your physiological state. Example: hunger, thirst, discomfort, etc.

Psychogenic needs arise on account of a person's specific need satisfaction relating to his psychological state of mind, which normally is not apparent. Example: satisfying the need for recognition, esteem, etc. In other words, biogenic needs refer to Maslow's physiological and safety needs while psychogenic needs refer to social, esteem and self-actualization need structures.

In psychological terms, cognitive dissonance is when a person feels and recognizes a discomfort due to conflicting ideas. In marketing, this emerges as buyer's remorse. Buyer's remorse (or cognitive dissonance) is when a person has second thoughts about whether they purchased the correct product. For example, a person may see a commercial for a product and be completely convinced that it is the best and immediately buy it. Later they see a commercial for a different brand of that product and are convinced that they have chosen wrong. They will then feel conflict. Either it will lead them to switch products, or they will decide that the commercial is wrong. Cognitive dissonance can also emerge after someone buys a large, expensive product, like a car. They may have really wanted the car when they bought it, but later realize that it was a little out of their price range.

THE CONCEPT OF FAMILY LIFECYCLE

There are seven stages in the lifecycle of a family and any buying activity is closely connected to the specific stage of the family life cycle present at that point of time:

Bachelor Stage: Young, single people – Few financial burdens. Fashion opinion leaders. Recreation-oriented. Buy: basic kitchen equipment, basic not living at home. Furniture, cars, equipment for the mating game, vacations.

Newly Married Couples: Young, no children – Better off financially than they will be in the near future. Highest purchase rate and highest average purchase of durables. Buy cars, refrigerators, stoves, sensible and durable furniture, and vacations.

Full Nest I: Youngest under six – Home purchasing at peak; liquid assets low. Dissatisfied with financial position and amount of money saved. Interested in new products. Buy washers, dryers, TV, baby food, baby medicines, dolls, and toys.

Full Nest II: Youngest child six or over – Financial position better. Some wives work. Less influenced by advertising. Buy larger-sized packages, multiple-unit deals. Buy many foods, cleaning materials, bicycles, music lessons, and pianos.

Full Nest III: Older couples with dependent children – Financial position still better. More wives work. Some children get jobs. Hard to influence with advertising. High average purchase of durables. Buy new, more tasteful furniture, auto travel, unnecessary appliances, boats, dental services, and magazines.

Empty Nest I: Older couples, no children living with them, head in labor force – Home ownership at peak. Most satisfied with financial position and money saved. Interested in travel, recreation, and self-education. Make gifts and contributions. Not interested in new products. Buy vacations, luxuries, and home improvements.

Empty Nest II: Older married couples, no children living at home, head retired – Drastic cut in income. Keep home. Buy medical appliances, medical-care products that aid health, sleep and digestion.

In addition to the family lifecycle, there are instances where a household will fall into one of the following situations:

Solitary Survivor, in Labor Force – Income still good but likely to sell home.

Solitary Survivor, Retired – Same medical and product needs as other retired group, drastic cut in income. Special need for affection, attention and security.

BUYING ROLES

There are five stages in any buying process. They are:

ORGANIZATIONAL, RESELLER AND GOVERNMENT MARKETS

ORGANIZATIONAL OR PRODUCER OR INDUSTRIAL MARKETS

The Organizational or Producer or Industrial Market is made up of business units that are engrossed in the manufacture of goods and services for sale or rental to other units. There are markets for raw materials, sub-assemblies, manufactured materials and parts, equipment, installations, accessories, services, etc. The Organizational buyer is interested in bottom lines unlike consumers who are interested in need satisfaction. They are extremely skilled buyers and know the markets thoroughly. Geographically they are concentrated, unlike a consumer buying process where a central person, though influenced by other members, makes the final decision. In Industrial or Production or Organizational buying, the buying process is carried out by several knowledgeable persons participating in it. A consumer buyer can have choices – like ordering a BigMac or plain sandwich. An organizational buyer has no choices. If only carbon steel is required for a manufacture, he has to get only carbon steel and not bronze. He is not interested in personal satisfaction like a consumer buyer because he is purchasing a product for further production of another product. The demand for organizational or industrial or producer's goods, therefore, is <u>derived</u> and not <u>primary</u>. Industrial goods are purchased by trained professionals, known as purchasing agents or buying agents. Another important characteristic of industrial goods is that the demand is mostly inelastic, i.e., it is not affected by any change in price. However, the degree of demand is largely related to the condition of the economy. In a boom period where consumers purchase products frequently and consistently, it is bound to affect supply, and therefore, the producers start purchasing more production machinery and raw materials to augment supplies so as to meet the consumers' increased demand. The increase in consumer demand generates a multiplier effect on the producer's goods. They purchase much more than required to meet the increased consumer demand.

Reseller Market: This market consists of individuals and organizations such as agents, selling intermediaries, distributors, wholesalers or dealers, who purchase goods with the sole intention of reselling or renting them to others in the market and achieving a good profit margin. Resellers handle a vast variety of goods for sale. A reseller faces such questions as:

- What assortment to carry in stock
- Who the vendor should be
- What price
- What terms

Any wholesaler or retailer can opt for any one of the four assortment strategies:

Reseller and the Buying Decision: Whether to involve in reselling activity of a new product or stay away depends upon the degree of profit the new product generates for the reseller. The greater the profit, the faster the involvement. Of course, the advertising backup, favorable credit terms and product utility are also taken into account. For an existing product, a reseller normally orders for stock when his inventory touches the reorder point.

The Government Markets: This comprises public sector undertakings that buy or rent goods for carrying out certain main functions of government, such as Federal, State, and Local governments, etc. Governments' buying is very huge. They buy from stationery to nuke materials and other items of warfare! Government buying procedures are highly specialized and in some cases cumbersome. Open bidding and negotiated contracts are employed in government buying. For standard items, open bidding procedure is used. The accredited government agency invites bids from qualified suppliers for very well specified items. The supplier who has quoted the lowest price is awarded the contract.

Organizing for Marketing Efforts

BASIC OBJECTIVES AND STRATEGIES

Demand Measurement: Success requires hard work. A company, if it wants to be very successful, must be able to measure the actual size of the market as of today and at a given future date. Quantitative Measurements are necessary to quantify an achievable target for the present year and for future years.

Market Demand: What is it? If you want to evaluate the Market Demand for a product, you have to take into account the total volume that you estimate to be bought by a predefined target audience in a given geographical area in a stated time frame within a given marketing environment covered by a clearly stated marketing program.

Market Forecast: The total market demand is likely to be in line with the marketing effort that a company is expected to put forth and this market demand that is assumed to be achieved is known as Market Forecast. The Market Forecast tells us the anticipated level of Market Demand for an anticipated degree of Marketing effort, happening in a given environment.

The Company Forecast: Every company anticipates a certain level of sales, during a given time period. It assumes what the marketing environment during that time period would be and it opts for a well thought out marketing plan to achieve such anticipated sales. This, in essence, is the company forecast. In other words, it is a company's planned, targeted sales for its products during a given time period. The plan assumes that there won't be any drastic changes in the environment.

Sales Quota: It is some sort of a sales goal for each salesman, each product of the product line, all company zones or regions or divisions, each distributor and each agent. It is a managerial tool for stimulating sales.

Sales Budget: It is a cautious estimate of sales during a given period based on the overall sales forecast meant mainly to arrive at the anticipated level of purchases, the level of production of each product and to help cash flow decisions.

Methods of Estimating – Current Demand: How to estimate current sales potential? There are two methods: (1) The breakdown method, and (2) The buildup method.

1. The Breakdown Method: The production and sales of any company is finally linked to the Economic Environment of a country. If the Economic Environment is good, it reflects on the production and sales levels of products – there is a boom everywhere. On the contrary if the Economic Environment of a country is really bad, again it reflects in the business gloom and there is a reduction in output and consequent dip in sales. The Economic Forecast of a country is the index as to whether the business should increase or decrease sales. A marketing company gets hold of the economic forecast for the next fiscal time period and estimates the level of sales potential on the basis of the economic forecast. The GNP forecast is broken down into Division, Distributor, Retailer, Salesmen and Products Sales.

2. The Buildup Method: It estimates the total number of units of all products marketed by the company which a typical buyer in a given sales territory during a given period is likely to purchase among various competing products. The number arrived at is then multiplied by the number of potential purchases in that particular territory. This procedure is followed for all territories of the company and the individual figure of each territory is totaled up to arrive at the anticipated market potential.

Methods of Estimating Future Demand: There are a number of methods and a company uses one or a combination of more than one such method to arrive at the future demand. The forecasting methods normally used to determine future demand are: surveys of what the buyer intends to buy, estimate of salesmen, expert opinions, conducting a market test for the product to solicit indications of future response of the purchaser, Statistical Demand Analysis and, of course, Time Series Analysis. Whether it is estimating current demand or future trends, care should be taken to collect pertinent data and information in an authentic manner.

Market Segmentation: No two people think alike. Likewise, no market is full of people who think alike, act alike, or buy alike. Tastes differ between individuals. All markets, therefore, are heterogeneous. A given product may be liked in one particular market and may not be selling in another. Even in a market where it sells well, there may be pockets where it sells extremely well and pockets where there may be not many sales. Marketing organizations with a view to overcome such shortcomings segment markets on a number of characteristics. The idea is to subdivide a market into homogenous subsets of customers. Any subset or a number of such subsets may be taken in as a target audience in that market and approached with a specific marketing mix. This is the underlying principle of segmentation. Let us learn about segmentations:

SEGMENTATION VARIABLES:

Geographic	Demographic	Psychographic	Benefit
Nation – Region State – Areas City Climate/ Terrain Population Density Density of the Market	Sex, Age, Amount of disposable income Spending Pattern Education Occupation Nationality Family	Social Class Lifestyle Personality Status Seekers Plain	Brand Loyalty Benefits Sought

There are other types of segmentations such as volume segmentation, marketing factor segmentation and product space segmentation.

STRATEGIES TOWARDS MARKET SEGMENTATION:

There are different strategies available to a marketing company towards Market segmentation:

1. **Undifferentiated Marketing:**
Only one product offered to hook all buyers. There may be only one Marketing Program.

Undifferentiated Marketing

2. **Differentiated Marketing:**
Separate products & separate marketing plan for individual segments.

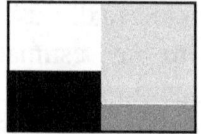
Differentiated Marketing

3. **Concentrated Marketing:**
Selects beneficial pockets of one or more segments and market, concentrating all the company's effort there. Instead of looking for a small share of a large market, opt for a large share of one or a few submarkets.

Concentrated Marketing

One aspect of marketing is how to consider the market. Often, products will have a target group, or segment, which can be classified through demographic, geographic, psychographic or behavioral characteristics.

Demographics is the study of populations, and therefore demographic segments are related to classifications of people within a population. This includes people with similar age, family situation, ethnicity, gender, jobs, income, religion or a number of other factors. For example, a children's pool is more applicable to families than it is to the market as a whole.

Geographic segmentation is segmentation based on location. This includes what part of the country a person is from, urban versus rural areas, and similarly sized metropolitan areas. For example, a snow shovel company would do better off advertising to northern states with lots of snow than it would to southern states with little snow.

Psychographic segments are segments with similar lifestyles. These are groups of people with similar activities, values, interests, personalities and opinions. For example, marketing guns or cooking supplies at trade shows geared to that sort of product. This way, the people who are most likely to purchase or want the product have the most access to it.

Behavioral segmentation is based on people's attitude toward the product. For example, if the person uses the product often, occasionally or rarely. This type of segmentation also plays off of brand loyalty and nearby occasions (if it's close to Christmas or Father's Day).

ORGANIZATIONAL OBJECTIVES AND STRATEGIES

Developing clear company objectives precedes a company's marketing planning. The objectives should spell out well thought out growth and competitive strategy. There are:

(1) Prime objectives (to aim for a stated end result high profit)

(2) Instrumental objectives (more basic aims to be accomplished – products, sales territories, salesmen, marketing instruments, etc.)

(3) Specific objectives (specific as to magnitude and time, average profit of about 15% over next 5 years, etc).

An organizational objective identifies employees with the organizational growth by providing a sense of purpose and work satisfaction. A well thought out objective may look like, "…to manufacture quality products that have the inherent characteristics for total customer satisfaction, provide a reasonable profit margin and aim for a greater market share…"

Robert Weinberg has the following basic strategic trade-offs each organization has to face:
1. Short term profits vs. long term profits
2. Profit margin vs. competitive position
3. Direct sales effort vs. market development effort
4. Penetration of existing markets vs. the development of new markets
5. Related vs. non-related new opportunities as a source of long-term growth
6. Profit vs. non-profit goals (social responsibilities)
7. Growth vs. stability
8. No risk environment vs. high risk environment

Objectives are a sort of statement of intent on where an organization would like to be, whereas strategies are grand designs aimed solely at getting the organization there.

1. <u>Market Penetration</u>: the company seeks increased sales for its present products in its present markets through more aggressive promotion and distribution.
2. <u>Market Development</u>: the company seeks increased sales by taking its present products into new markets.
3. <u>Product Development</u>: the company seeks increased sales by developing improved products for its present markets.
4. <u>Diversification</u>: the company seeks increased sales by developing new products for new markets. This is not an intensive strategy.

MARKETING ORGANIZATION

Every business unit has a variety of complex tasks to be performed and. Therefore. requires men, machines, materials, money, and of course data and info. Marketing, in a basic setup, is all about order generation. The supply tasks are something like this in a basic setup.

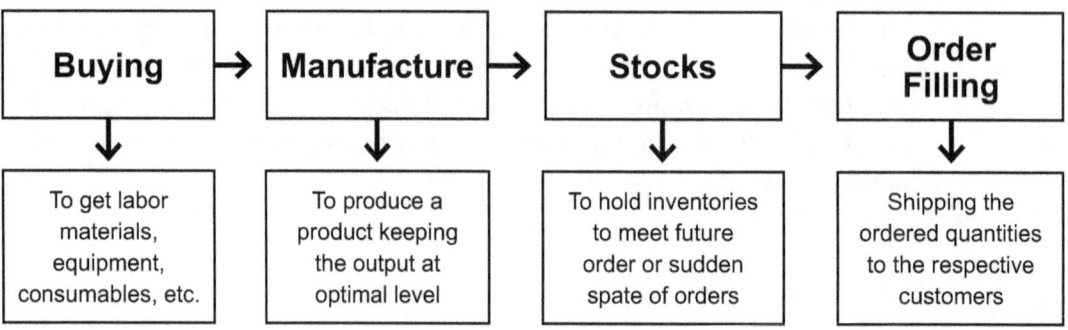

A function-oriented marketing organization will look like:

A product-oriented marketing organization will look like:

A centralized marketing organization will look like:

In decentralized marketing organizations, other than corporate marketing – corporate advertisement – corporate marketing research, which are common, the North Division will have General Manager, Marketing Manager and North's separate advertisement and sales team plus marketing research. They, of course, work within the overall corporate parameter set by corporate marketing.

TYPES OF PLANNING IN MARKETING

What is planning? To put it simply, it is deciding <u>today</u> what you should do <u>tomorrow</u>. Planning is deciding at the present moment to achieve a stated objective in a predetermined future spelling out in clear terms how to go about it. How and where to start? It is better to study what Philip Kotler, the undisputed marketing guru has said in his epoch of a book, "…Marketing Management – Analysis, Planning and Control…"

"…Diagnosis: where is the company now, and why?

Prognosis: where is the company headed?
Objectives: where should the company be headed?
Strategy: what is the best way to get there?

Tactics: what specific actions should be undertaken, by whom and when?
Control: what measures should be watched to indicate whether the company is succeeding?..."

The above questions lead you to the present state of affairs of the company, where is it heading, actually where you want it to go, how to get there, what are the tactics and who will ensure that the company is on the right track.

TYPES OF PLANNING IN MARKETING

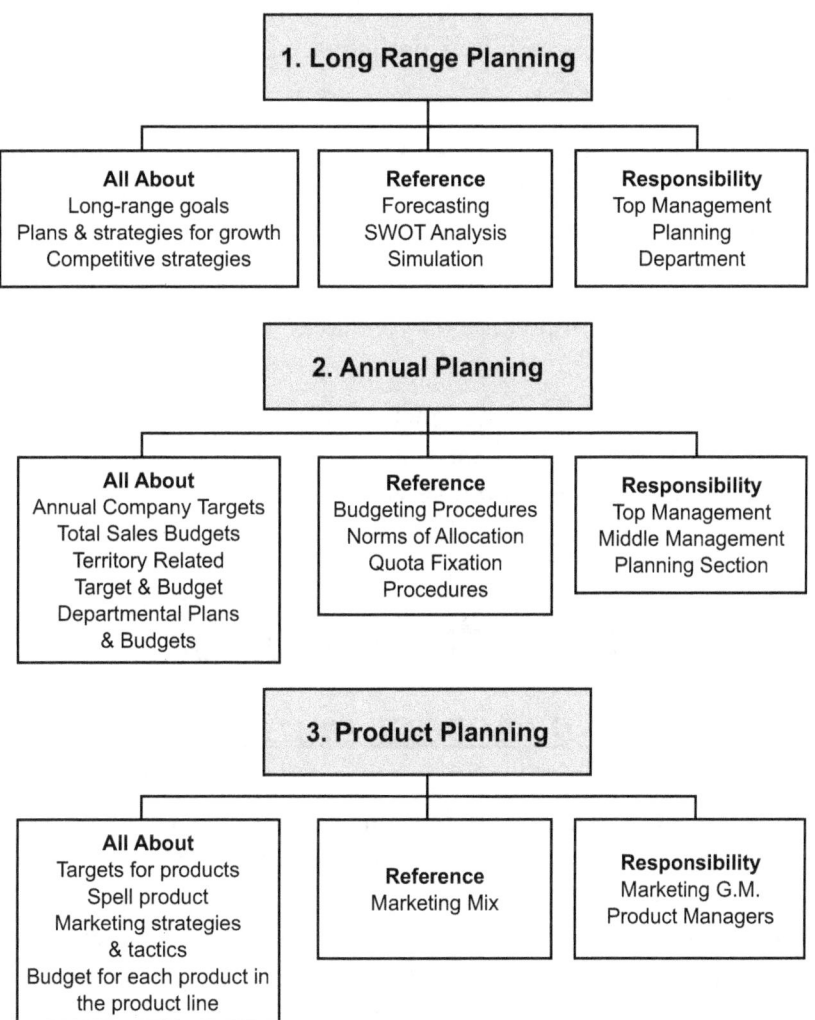

SWOT ANALYSIS

SWOT Analysis is a very important part of marketing. SWOT is a way to identify your strengths and weaknesses. SWOT stands for:

- Strengths
    - What are your advantages?
    - What makes you unique?
    - What resources do you have?

- Weaknesses
  - Where do you need to improve? Do you have customer service problems, high refund rates, cash flow problems, etc?
- Opportunities
  - What outside opportunities do you have? Has your industry recently been mentioned in the press? Have you discovered a new niche or market segment?
- Threats
  - What outside competition do you have? What obstacles do you face?

SWOT analysis can give you a clear picture of where your company is, where it is going and how you can get there. This is a very useful tool for marketing as it can discover new ways to position and promote your product.

Planning and Marketing Mix

TYPES OF PRODUCTS AND PRODUCT TRAITS

The Tangible Products: The physical products or services offered. Example: lipstick, televisions, computers, typing services, educational programs, etc.

The Extended Product: Physical products – tangible products – together with a gamut of services going with the products. A computer is a tangible product accompanied with a host of services like software, hardware instructions, canned software programs, maintenance, important parts like hard drive guarantees and peripheral supplies, making it an extended product. Tangible product + accompanying services, guarantees, freebies = Extended Product.

The Generic Products: It relates to the buyer's expectations of basic benefits the product is supposed to shower on the buyer. Example: a computer. The buyer is not interested in the hardware or software or peripherals. He is acquiring a computer for problem solving abilities. A computer, therefore, is a generic product of problem solving. A nail polish is a generic product of beauty.

The BCG Growth Share Matrix can be used to classify products based on their market growth rate and relative market share. Market growth rate is how quickly the particular market is growing. For example, in technology, there is always something newer and better, meaning high growth and a lot of money to be made. However, as far as grocery stores go, there are always going to be the same basic products, and people will be buying the same basic things. This means there is low growth. Relative market share is how prominent the product is within the market. For example, stores like Walmart and Target tend to dominate the grocery industry with large market shares, whereas local based stores have a low market share. Based on how the products rate in these two categories, they can be called a dog, problem child, star or cash cow.

A dog is a product with low market growth and low relative market share. It is a product in a slowly growing industry with little recognition. It may break even as far as costs go, but it doesn't have any real potential and ties up a lot of resources for a company. Financially speaking, they are worthless assets.

A problem child, or question mark, is a product with a low relative market share in a fast growing market. Because the market is growing fast, they have a lot of potential to do well, but the low relative market share means that they could fall into the dog category if or when the market slows down. If they gain market share, they could move into the star or cash cow category.

A star is a product with a high market share in a fast growing industry. These are products that lead in their market, and generate a lot of revenue. However, it may require a lot of money to keep the product at the front of their market. When the market slows down, there is potential for them to fall to a dog if the product doesn't keep a high market share, but if they do keep a high market share they become cash cows.

A cash cow is a product with a high market share in a slow growing industry. In other words, it is one of the most recognized products in a field that doesn't sustain much change. This is the best type of product to have because it allows the company to make a lot of money, with little investment needed (at this point marketing isn't really necessary). It generates the revenue needed to keep the company functioning, and possibly allow them to expand and turn problem child and star products into cash cows as well.

THE PRODUCT MIX DECISIONS

Before we proceed to take up product mix decisions, let us see what PLC is – Product Life Cycle.

Product Life Cycle: The systematic study of a product's history will reveal a varying cycle of stages of opportunities and threats, ups and downs that are relevant to any marketing strategy. There are distinct stages in a product's PLC known as Introduction, Growth, Maturity and Decline.

THE STAGES OF PRODUCT LIFE CYCLE

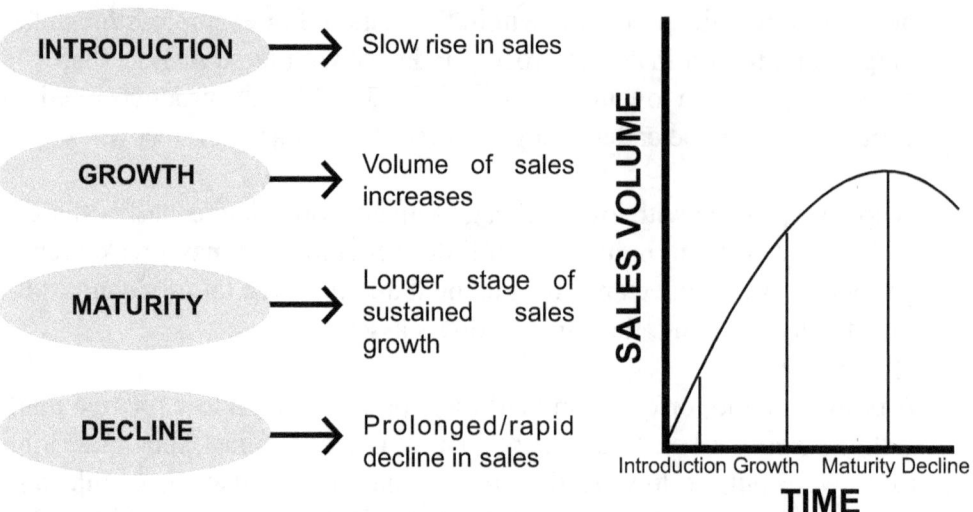

The particular stage at which a product is at the time of preparing the Marketing strategy, has a lot to do with the allocation for each element of the Marketing Mix. The PLC can also be applied to a Product <u>Class</u> (say perfumes) or to a specific <u>Brand</u> (say Christian Dior or Intimate) or to a product <u>Form</u> (say sprays, roll-ons, etc.). The product policy decisions of a company are taken at three different levels as each company today produces products at a prolific rate.

<u>Product Item</u>: A particular version of a product. Example: Sony 'Walkman II'.

<u>Product Line</u>: A group of closely related products. Example: All Walkman products of Sony.

<u>Product Mix</u>: A number of related products offered. Sony's 'Walkman', HiFi products, etc.

Now let us study the 'width,' 'depth' and 'consistency' of the product mix.

<u>Width</u>: Refers to the number of product lines offered. Mitsubishi produces a range of products from air conditioners, machines, electric appliances, cars, etc.

<u>Depth</u>: Refers to the average number of products offered within each product line. LG produces air conditioning machines with different capacities 0.5 ton, 1.0 ton, 1.5 tons, 2.0 ton, split AC, etc.

<u>Consistency</u>: How similarly related the offered product lines end use, production and distribution. A product line of air conditioners is related in that they all involve electricity. The Product Life Cycle concept has close links with the Adoption and Diffusion processes. The adoption process has a tendency to affect the length of a given product's Life Cycle. Let us now see how a new product is adopted.

The Adoption Process: Unless some buyer buys a product in its introductory stage of PLC, it cannot survive that stage. The adoption processes are a series of stages a potential buyer is likely to go through in order to decide to buy a product and also continue to use the product. There are four stages:

AWARENESS	Knows about the product but has no data or info
INTEREST	Seeks info
EVALUATION	Weighing mentally the advantages and disadvantages of the new product
TRIAL	Effects a trial purchase in order to see for himself the usefulness of the offered product
ADOPTION	Becomes a customer by using the product regularly

The Adoption Rate depends on:

(1) Relative advantage – product's superiority over others

(2) Compatibility – product's consistency in relation to the buyer's cultural value and lifestyle

(3) Complexity – the relative difficulty in understanding or using the offered product

(4) Divisibility – degree to which the product is allowed for trial use

(5) Communicability – observed product behavior results communicated to others by word of mouth

If the communicability aspect is greater, the chances of the product's adoption rate are faster.

The Diffusion Process: How fast a new product spreads throughout a target market is known as the Diffusion Process. There are 5 categories of adopters. They are:

1. Innovators
2. Early adopters
3. Early majority
4. Late majority
5. Laggards

A bell curve will give us a clear picture about the diffusion process:

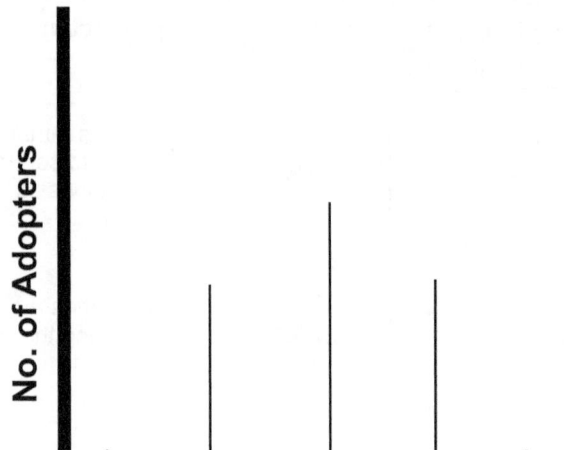

Time of Adoption

From the above you can see that the innovators and early adopters together account for only (2.5 +13.5) = 16%. In other words, those who have not yet adopted the product are still a majority – 84%. However, if innovators and early adopters do not adopt, even though they only adopt 16%, the chances of others trying the product are nil and consequently the product is bound to fail in the market.

CHANNELS OF DISTRIBUTION

The American Marketing Association defines the channel of distribution as: "…an organized network of agencies and institutions, which in combination perform all the activities required to link producers with users to accomplish the marketing task…" If any organization really wants to enter a competitive market, its options are: (1) Induce independent channels to promote the organization's products by giving incentives (2) Establish their own franchised outlets.

No product will reach the market unless there is a well thought out distribution system. To do this, it is necessary to bring in the services of intermediaries in order to effect a foolproof product distribution system. A channel of distribution is a series of institutions dealing in marketing activities, which facilitates transfers of the goods as well as the title to goods from producer to other intermediaries to the ultimate consumer. Let us consider the normal channel employed for both consumer and producer goods.

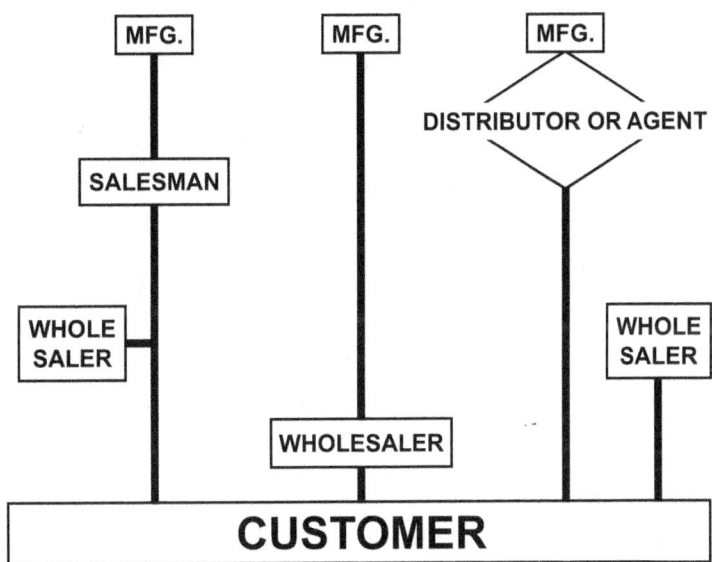

If you want an effective channel, your approach should be to find out what the customer really wants and based on that develop your strategy. Which are the factors that influence channel development?

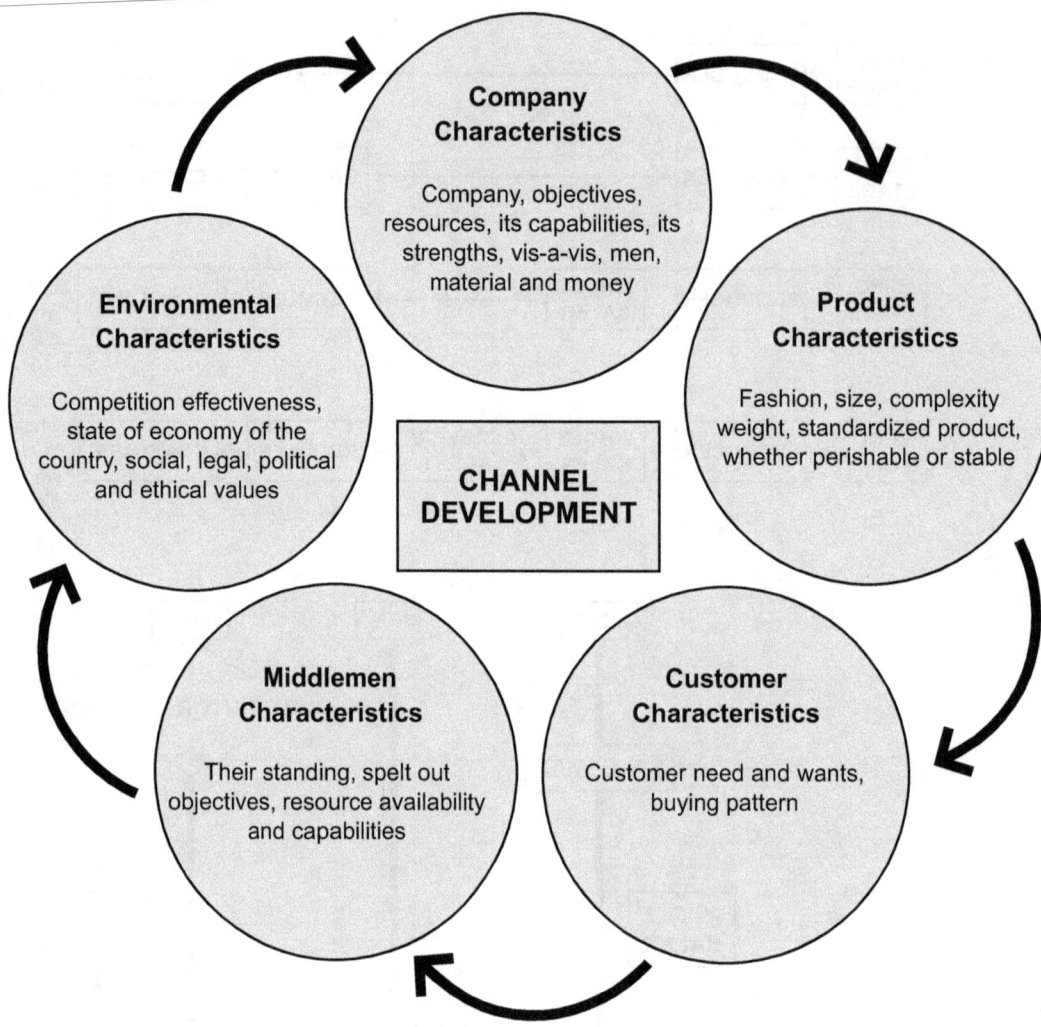

Channel Planning: (1) Should know the type of middlemen required, (2) Number of such middlemen in each type, (3) Which particular middlemen to use, and, (4) How to motivate middlemen.

1. Determining Types of Middlemen:
Dual Distribution: If a unit uses two or more competing channels for its sales of product lines it is known as a Dual Distribution system. Example: Using company outlets and retail outlets.

Facilitating Middlemen: Producer moves goods and title to goods to the ultimate buyer. Transporter moves goods, Bankers finance, Insurers insure the inventory in transit and Marketing Research firms provide information. They are functional middlemen and are known as facilitating middlemen. Channel members use such facilitating middlemen if they are convinced they can carry out all the functions more economically and most efficiently.

2. The Number of Middlemen to Use:
This largely depends on whether you want (a) an intensive (b) selective or (c) exclusive distributor.
   (a) Intensive Distribution: Product to be available in as many outlets as possible. Example: soaps, detergents or cigarettes.
   (b) Selective Distribution: Related to distribution in a geographic area restricted to middlemen guided by their perceived performance capability. Industrial products, specialized products and shopping products are distributed on selective distribution basis.
   (c) Exclusive Distribution: Having only one exclusive outlet in a geographic area. Some specialty products like Leica Cameras, Rolex watches are distributed on the basis of exclusive distribution.

3. Which Particular Middlemen to Use:
Producers can choose whichever middlemen they like provided the middlemen are willing, capable and ever ready to participate in the channel.

4. How to Motivate Middlemen:
Trade promotions, selective promotional allowances to take care of advertising costs, publicity, and good use of product displays – all these are some of the motivational tools used by producers to make middlemen work better. Additionally, a salesman's rapport with the middlemen goes a long way in motivating middlemen.

Personal Selling
In the realm of personal selling (selling things in person) two of the main theories are missionary selling and relationship selling. Missionary selling involves seeking out new customers and convincing them to buy the product for the first time. This would be done, for example, by door to door salespeople. The idea is to convince the buyer to have faith in the product (which is where the name came from). Generally, this approach is considered to consume more time, energy and resources than its alternate, relationship selling. Relationship selling follows the theory that it is easier to maintain a client than to find a new one. The idea is to start a genuine relationship with the client, to listen to their needs and concerns, so that they will keep coming back.

Retailing
Retailing is when a store front is opened to sell goods to the end user or consumer. Examples of these are companies such as Walmart, Target, grocery stores, etc. Sometimes these lower-end retailers use a concept called the **wheel of retailing.**

Some retailers enter the market with low cost, low margin and low status companies. Over time, they add value added services, more products, and upgrade their facilities along with their prices. Eventually they get more status and evolve into a household name or brand. However, these higher operating expenses leave them vulnerable to other new companies that come into the marketplace at the beginning of the cycle.

E-Commerce
The buying and selling of goods and services over the internet is referred to as e-commerce. There are four general formats through which e-commerce occurs:

- Business to Business (B2B)
- Business to Consumer (B2C)
- Consumer to Business (C2B)
- Consumer to Consumer (C2C)

The first form of e-commerce, B2B, includes situations in which businesses interact over the internet. If a grocery store, which is a business, finds and pays for boxes of cereal from a manufacturer, which is also a business, over the internet then it would be an example of B2B e-commerce.

The second form B2C is the one that most people would think of. This is when companies sell products over the internet. For example, many large supermarket chains also offer a full array of products which can be purchased online and delivered to customer's homes. Some companies even exist exclusively online.

The third form of e-commerce, C2B, occurs when consumers post their payment offers or budgets for goods or services online, and businesses decide whether they are willing to accept at that price. In this way consumers can make offers to multiple companies at once without having to negotiate with them individually.

The final form of e-commerce, C2C, describes sites which allow for direct negotiation between consumers. For example, online auction sites which allow individuals to post products they wish to sell, and search for products they wish to buy.

International Business
Importing and exporting are how countries trade goods and services with each other. An export is produced in one country and sold to another. Exports are a small percent of GDP for the U.S. unlike for countries such as Germany and the United Kingdom. Imports are currently how we spend 20% of our money – and it is steadily increasing.

Trade barriers are anything that makes it difficult (or creates ad barrier) to trade. One natural barrier to trade is distance. This increases the cost to transport a product. Another barrier is language. If you cannot communicate with your buyer, then you cannot initiate or complete a transaction. A protectionist is someone who proclaims "buy American". Their primary aim is to keep jobs, companies and industries inside the country. Currently, there is a lot of coverage in the news about jobs being outsourced to India.

A tariff is a duty or a tax that a government puts on products that are imported or exported from a country. Sometimes a country enacts an embargo. An embargo is a prohibition or suspension of a certain type of item, or anything from a certain country or region. For example, the U.S. has an embargo against ivory and some types of firearms. Each country chooses their own items (if any) on which to place an embargo.

While it is considered a legal form of trade restrictions and is not an act of war (that would be a blockade), an embargo is a strong diplomatic policy and is often used to send a message. Embargoes do not necessarily have to be all inclusive, but can be limited to specific products. For example, an embargo on flour would mean that a company could not import or export any flour. On the other hand, an embargo on trade with a certain country would mean that all products could still be exported or imported, just not to and from that specific country.

GATT is the General Agreement on Tariffs and Trade is a treaty designed to reduce trade barriers. NAFTA is the North American Free Trade Agreement which helps reduce trade barriers between the United States, Canada and Mexico. The primary purpose of NAFTA is to lower trading barriers and dealing with trade disputes. Basically, NAFTA created a free trade zone between the three countries. NAFTA is governed by three Secretariats (one from each country), and creates a method through which trade disputes between the three countries can be resolved.

The World Bank is a part of the United Nations that provides loans to countries for development projects. IMF is the International Monetary Fund, an agency that seeks to establish a way for countries to finance and pay off loans. IMF is affiliated with the World Bank.

A bill of lading is a document of title which is a contract between the shipper and the carrier (think you and FedEx). It also serves as a receipt for the products that the shipper has placed on the carrier.

When a company exports more than it imports, it is considered a favorable balance of trade. This is referred to as a **trade surplus** (because the country is bringing in more money from abroad than it is spending). In this case, net exports would be positive. On the other hand, if a country imports more than it exports, the result is an unfavorable balance of trade referred to as a trade deficit. In the case of a trade deficit, the value of net exports is negative.

The value of the products a nation exports minus the value of the products they import is referred to as the balance of trade or net exports. The balance of trade is always measured over a specific period of time. For example, the United States generally measures its net exports over the period of a year. If a country were to import 20 billion dollars of goods and services in a year, and exported 30 billion dollars of goods and services in a year, then **net exports** would be 10 million dollars.

PRODUCT PROMOTION EFFORTS

Promotion is a company's attempt to generate sales through effective communication to any group of buyers. The forms of promotion are: advertising, personal selling, sales promotion and publicity.

Now let us suppose you have an excellent product with all the attributes needed, with a price tag that is attractive, and with a system that makes the product easily available to the consumer. You have advantages of product, price and distribution. Will this situation generate excellent sales? The answer is a definite no! If a company wants to generate exceptional sales, it must spend time in creating a meaningful and effective program of communication and promotion. Communication is a process of influencing other's behavior pattern. So, it is communication – meaningful and effective communication that is the basic building block of any promotional activity. A communication model consists of:

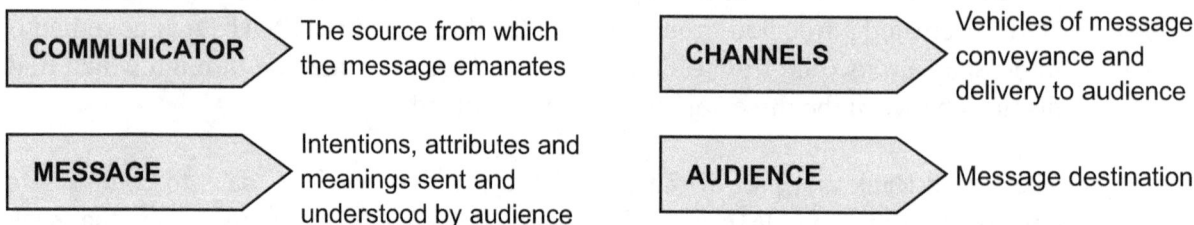

To make a purchase, a buyer has to be influenced and an effective communication does just that. There are channels of influence and let us see them now:

CHANNELS OF INFLUENCE

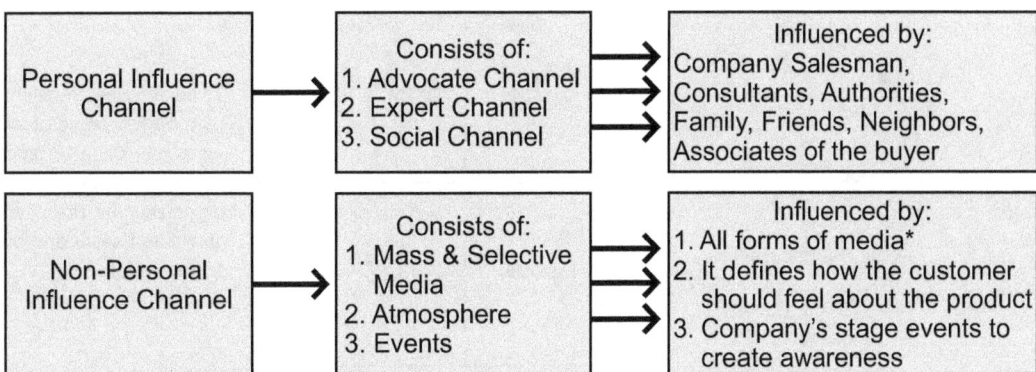

* (A) Print media like newspapers, magazines; Broadcast media like radio, television; Information technology media like websites, emails, etc. (B) Outdoor media like billboards, etc.

Message: Meaningful and effective communication needs (1) to identify the target audience, and (2) which channels to use in order to reach the target audience. The designing of the message should be in keeping with the target audience and selected channels. According to John C. Maloney: "…is advertising believability really important…" "…No single advertisement is likely to produce absolute 'belief' in a product. Rather each advertisement is likely to make its most significant contribution by nudging the consumer onto and along the path of the adoption process…"

Vertical channels occur when all the levels of production and distribution for a product are owned by the same person. For example, it would be a vertical channel if a person owns the factory their product is made in, a trucking store to ship it around the country and retail stores to sell the product in. This creates a channel through which the product is produced.

Horizontal channels are all essentially on the same level of production. For example, a Walmart store often has a McDonald's store in them. Both are on the same level because they sell directly to a consumer, and, although they are entirely different stores, they both benefit from teaming up together. For example, horizontal channels also occur when a number of factories merge.

THE PROMOTION MIX

A promotion mix consists of (1) Personal Selling (2) Advertising (3) Sales Promotion, and (4) Public Relations. Some have included packaging also in the promotion mix but considering it as an essential extension and attribute of a product, it can safely be taken as an extended product form rather than part of a product mix.

PROMOTION MIX IN A NUTSHELL

Personal Selling: Ensures face to face contact between company's salesman and the buyer. A good salesman who enjoys good personal rapport with a buyer can achieve exceptional results.

Advertising: Helps to identify the needed products

Sales Promotion: Programs designed to directly or indirectly stimulate sales

Sales: Sales contests, consumer contests, discount sales, etc.

Publicity: Publicity is to maintain good will as well as to create a favorable impression about the company and its products.

Brief Objectives of Promotions:
1. To create awareness
2. To provide information about the company and its products
3. To explain company programs
4. To induce a buyer for a product trial
5. Coaxing middlemen to stock products
6. To create customer loyalty
7. Try to reduce seasonal fluctuation by offering special programs during off season

There are two different ways to promote a product: push strategy and pull strategy. To push a product involves bringing the product to the customer, and making sure they are aware of it. The developers market it to the manufacturers who market it to the stores who market it to the buyers.

They may put up window displays or offer special deals, anything to get the buyer to become aware of the product. Pull strategy involves bring the customer to the product. This strategy involves creating a demand for the product that will pull it through the stages. For example, if there is a TV commercial advertising the product, people will request it in the stores. The stores will then seek the product from manufacturers and so on.

ADVERTISING

Methods of marketing include direct and indirect marketing. Direct marketing involves a hands on approach. Internet ads, newspaper ads, TV commercials, telemarketers and coupons are all types of direct advertising. Anything which is done by the company to directly generating demand and interest in their products is considered direct advertising. Indirect advertising, on the other hand, is harder to pin down. This is when advertising occurs, but in a less forceful way. For example, word of mouth advertising is when a person recommends a product they like. Also, if a company donates money to a cause and their name is listed, it is also a form of indirect advertising.

Advocacy advertising is advertising which is designed to support one side of a controversial issue. Essentially, it is advertising a person's viewpoint and they are trying to persuade others of their position. An example would be if a person puts a large sign in their yard advocating a political candidate. Or, if a person writes an article advocating gun control.

PRICE DETERMINATION

Macroeconomic theory, as well as general equilibrium theory, emphasizes the predominance of price theory in economics for over a century now. However, in today's business, so many variables such as household consumption increase in the disposable income pattern of people, agricultural, industrial, electronics and knowledge revolutions all put their stamps on the pricing mechanism of companies all over the world. The non-pricing variables are to be studied and dealt with in your overall price determination.

Where do pricing decisions assume significance?

If a unit sets a price for the first time when a new product is introduced, there is always an uncertainty on the pricing front. Likewise, if a unit introduces a product into a new and untried market segment, it has a problem at hand.

When a unit has to consider initiating a price revision, it has to face uncertainties. The price change may be on account of sudden demand fluctuations or increased costs.

Again if a competitor initiates a revision in price, the unit has no choice except to toe the line or face erosion in sales.

If a unit produces many products interrelated by costs or demands, the pricing decision becomes a real problem. How to determine an optimal price relationship for the individual products in the product line? It is definitely a mind-boggling problem.

PRICE ELASTICITY

A price elasticity of -1 tells us that sales will rise/fall by an identical percentage change as price falls/rises. Likewise, a price elasticity of which is greater than -1 indicates that sales will rise/fall by such percentage point that is more than the price fall/rise. And finally, a price elasticity of less than -1 tell us that sales will rise/fall by less than price falls/rises in terms of percentage.

In the first case, there won't be any change in the total revenue. In the second case, the total revenue is likely to rise. And in the third case, there is bound to be a total revenue fall. This is a most important factor every company has to bear in mind before attempting any revision in product price.

What are the objectives in price fixing?

1. **Market Penetration Objective:** They start with relatively low price, in order to obtain a bigger market share. Any market which is price sensitive can offer a better sales volume with a small cut in price. Also, they resort to this objective if they are facing potential competition whose efforts the company has to nullify.

2. **Market Skimming Objective:** In any market, there are buyers who are willing to pay a higher price if they perceive the value of the product is more compared to other products. Also, if they find that a higher price tag has no imminent danger of coaxing competition to enter in a big way.

3. **Early Recovery Objective:** The pricing is done in such a way that the company is assured of rapid recovery of cash.

4. **Satisfying Objective:** A satisfactory rate of return is aimed through this pricing objective.

5. **Product Line Promotion Objective:** It is possible that setting a price for a product, even at a small loss, increases the volume of sales of the complete product line. They refer to this pricing objective as "loss-leader" pricing.

One way of characterizing the demand for goods is as either elastic or inelastic. When the demand for a good is elastic, this means it is determined on price. For example, the demand for candy tends to be elastic because people only want to buy it if it is inexpensive, and the demand for it goes down if it becomes expensive. Inelastic products are products that people will buy no matter what the cost. Gas is one such product. Although people complain about rising prices, they still buy it because they need it.

PRICING MODELS

1. **Cost-Oriented Pricing:** It is normally covering all costs, which includes an arbitrary allocation of overhead as a percentage of operating costs.

2. **Markup Pricing:** The important mark-up pricing is cost-plus pricing in which a certain fixed percentage is added to the product cost. It is common in retail business.

3. **Target Pricing:** It is a pricing practice in which price is determined on the basis of a specified target rate of return on the total costs arrived at on the basis of an estimated standard volume.

4. **Demand-Oriented Pricing:** It is a simple economic pricing where a higher price is charged when there is a heavy demand and a reduced price charged when the demand slips.

5. **Price Discrimination:** A particular product is marketed at two or more prices either on the basis of customer, or on the basis of product version (products vary with slight variations) or, on the basis of place (theater seats are place-based price discrimination).

6. **Competition-Oriented Pricing:** The company waits for competitors to make the first move and then follows in the price revision.

7. **Going Rate Pricing (Imitative Pricing):** It is a type of competition oriented-pricing where a unit holds its price at an average level charged by the industry.

8. **Sealed Bid Pricing:** It is also a type of competition oriented pricing where companies compete on the basis of bids. Example: original equipment manufacturers, defense contracts, public work contracts, etc.

MARKUP

Markup is the difference between the actual price of the product to the store and the price they sell the product for. In other words, markup is the difference between wholesale price and retail price. Markup can be determined as either a percentage or an actual value. For example, if the wholesale price of a product is $10 and it is sold by the store for $20, the markup is $10 or 100%. It is 100% because the price doubled, or the $10 added is the total wholesale price. Also, if the wholesale price of an item was $100 and the markup percentage was 25%, the retail price would be $125.

BREAK-EVEN POINT

The break-even point is where the cost of producing a product equals the profit made from selling it. For example, it might cost a company $30,000 dollars to produce 5,000 couches. If they only sell 4,000 couches, they will have lost a lot of money. If they sell 6,000 couches they will make a lot of money. However, if they sell 5,000 couches they will break even. They won't have lost any money, but they won't have made any money. To calculate the break-even point you must determine total costs, which includes fixed costs and variable costs, and total revenue.

Fixed costs are costs which are incurred once and don't change. For example, a factory buys a new machine. They only pay for that machine once. On the other hand, variable costs are the cost that is incurred with each new unit of product produced. For example, a taffy factory buys their machine (the fixed cost) but for each sheet of taffy they produce, they have to buy ingredients.

For example, a toy factory, just going into business, buys two machines at $3,000 each. For each toy they produce, they must pay 75 cents. However, they sell the toys for five dollars. Assume that there are no other costs to the business, and that the business will sell all the products it makes.

To determine how many toys they must sell to break even, the formula would be: (Variable Costs * Volume) + Total Costs = (Price * Volume) The total cost would be $6,000 + 0.75x. The total revenue would be $5x (x will represent the number of toys produced and the number sold because we want them to be equal).

Therefore, the equation is:

$6,000 + $0.75x = $5x
$6,000 = $5x − $0.75x
x = $6,000/ ($5-$0.75)
x= 1,411.8

The business must sell at least 1,412 toys to break even.

MARKETING EFFORT CONTROL

Any effort needs control. Without control you do not know whether your efforts are bearing fruit as desired. Without control you know not whether you are on the track or off the track or heading in the right direction or in the opposite.

A marketing control sub-system aims to control the efficiency of its sales team, the efficiency of its advertising effectiveness, the efficiency of its distribution channel effectiveness, the efficiency of its product transportation effectiveness, and the effectiveness of its annual plans and monthly targets. Let us now see the 4 elements of a control system:

The most important control measures are aimed at expense and revenue deviation analysis of which the ratio analysis is essential. Some of the ratio analysis that gives you a fair picture of the "goings on" thereby presenting you with a platform for corrective action are:

(1) Expense to sales ratios (cost per sales call, cost incurred to prospect, advertisement expenses to sales, etc).
(2) Sales to gross profit ratios.
(3) Percentage of returned goods.
(4) Current sales to order backlog ratios.
(5) Individual salesman turnover.
(6) Number of months inventory held in factory and in distributor's warehouse.
(7) Bad debts ratio.

ABC analysis of sales concentration (i.e., sales percentage of top 20 percent customers), etc. A standard control chart model can be gainfully employed to control expenses.

From the above chart you can see that the ratio of expenses to sales is within the targeted level most of the target period, but during the final stages of the target period, it goes beyond the upper control limit, which is likely to happen as towards the end there will be a spurt in activity to reach overall targets.

The Seven Steps of Selling

- **Prospect for Leads:** You need to find people that want/need/can't live without your product. This can be the end user/consumer if you are selling used cars, or the buyer for your local Walmart store.

- **Preapproach:** Determine what their needs are. Do your research and make an appointment.

- **Qualify the Prospect/Approach:** Determine what the best way to sell your product to that particular person or group is. What is their motivation in buying the product? Is this person the decision maker? What need are you trying to fill? A dentist selling their services will market to young parents much differently than they would to a 70-year-old retiree.

- **Make the Presentation:** You are not only selling the product; you are selling yourself. Be on time, make eye-contact and be prepared.

- **Address any Objections:** Be able to turn any objection into a selling point for the customer. Be prepared to address any concern, such as price, portability, ease of use, etc.

- **Close the Sale:** Ask for the sale. Don't leave without the order or asking what you can do to earn their business.

- **Ask for Referrals/Follow Up:** Once the sale is done, follow up. Not only ensure that their needs were met but ask for referrals to other customers.

Writing a Marketing Plan

Writing and creating a marketing plan takes you through every step of the process of taking a new product to market, if done correctly. Now we'll take some of the information we've already learned about and put it into practice, while learning some new things along the way.

AOSTC is a tool for creating marketing plans:

Analysis
Objectives
Strategies
Tactics
Controls

The first step, analysis includes the SWOT test, as well as, other important factors like political climate, trends, laws and regulations, etc.

The second step objective is where you need to create objectives using the SMART test. **SMART** stands for:

Specific
Measurable
Achievable
Realistic
Timed

The third step is creating a strategy. What is the target market that you are going after? What is the demographic? What makes this segment the best?

The fourth step is tactics. This is where the Four P's come into play again.

Price
Place
Product
Promotion

Determine the specifics of each category.

Price – Will the product be at, above or below the competition?

Place – How will the product be sold or distributed?

Product – Are there any special features? Will it be bundled?

Promotion – How will it be marketed? Online? Through retailers? Direct mail?

The fifth step is controls. These refer to the hard aspects of running any business or campaign such as market date, startup costs, production costs, commissions, etc.

Legal Aspects of Marketing

LEGISLATION

The Sherman Antitrust Act was passed in 1890 and was the first act to work against monopolies (or trusts) and cartels. It made it illegal for any contract, deal, conspiracy or scheme to restrain trade, and allowed the government the right to investigate and take legal action against any company that did. This would therefore include when large companies formed cartels to drive up prices, or when one company grew large enough to put all others out of business. The law wasn't really recognized until the presidency of Theodore Roosevelt who became known as a "trustbuster" for using it to bring down major monopolies.

The Clayton Act (or Clayton Antitrust Act) was passed in 1914 as an amendment to the Sherman Antitrust Act to clarify the prohibited actions. For example, it specifically mentioned local price cuts (lowering the price in only one area to put competition out of business and then raising prices) and exclusive sales contracts. It also legalized strikes and boycotts.

The Robinson-Patman Act was passed in 1936 and amended the Clayton Act. The act had specifically mentioned local price cuts, but the Robinson-Patman Act extended it to include other forms of price discrimination. The main focus was on price discrimination from wholesalers to retailers. Chain stores, because of their size, were often able to get the same products for cheaper and were able to profitably undersell their competition. The act made it illegal for wholesalers to sell a product for less to one store than another. Because of this it is often referred to as the "chain store act."

The Federal Trade Commission Act was passed in 1914. It prevents companies from using unfair or deceptive business practices, and gives the government the right to issue cease and desist orders. It created the Federal Trade Commission (FTC), a five-person board created to regulate unfair business practices. Members of the FTC are appointed for overlapping seven year terms and no more than three members can be from the same party.

TAXES

Tariffs are taxes levied on goods imported from (or exported to) another country. Typically, this is done for two reasons: to make locally made goods more attractive and to increase government revenue. The reason that tariffs make locally made goods more attractive is because it means that the foreign products have the added expense, and it helps allow the locally made good to be priced lower. However, sometimes it can still be cheaper to buy those products even with the added tax.

The North American Free Trade Agreement (NAFTA) established one of the largest free trade zones in the world. It eliminated almost all tariffs between trade through Canada, the United States and Mexico.

 # Online Marketing

In today's digital age, online marketing has become an essential component of any successful marketing strategy. As more and more people spend time online, businesses have recognized the importance of reaching their target audience through various digital channels. This comprehensive guide will delve into the key aspects of online marketing, including banner ads, cost per click, impressions, conversions, remarketing, and click-through rates.

BANNER ADS

Banner ads are one of the most common forms of online advertising. These are graphical advertisements that are displayed on websites, typically in the form of a rectangular image or a video. Banner ads are designed to attract attention and encourage users to click on them, which directs them to the advertiser's website or landing page.

Banner ads come in various sizes and formats, such as static images, animated graphics, or interactive rich media. The effectiveness of banner ads depends on several factors, including the ad's design, placement, and relevance to the target audience.

COST PER CLICK (CPC)

Cost Per Click (CPC) is a pricing model used in online advertising, where advertisers pay each time a user clicks on one of their ads. This model is commonly used in search engine advertising, such as Google Ads, where advertisers bid on specific keywords and pay whenever a user clicks on their ad.

The cost per click varies depending on the competition for the targeted keywords and the advertiser's quality score, which is determined by factors such as the relevance and quality of the ad and the landing page. Advertisers can set a maximum CPC bid, which is the highest amount they are willing to pay for a single click.

IMPRESSIONS

Impressions refer to the number of times an ad is displayed, regardless of whether it is clicked on or not. In online marketing, impressions are used to measure the reach of an ad campaign. The more impressions an ad receives, the more people have seen it.

Impressions are important because they help advertisers gauge the visibility of their ads and determine whether they are reaching their target audience. However, impressions alone do not necessarily translate into clicks or conversions, which are more important metrics for measuring the success of an ad campaign.

CONVERSIONS

Conversions are the ultimate goal of most online marketing campaigns. A conversion occurs when a user takes a desired action, such as making a purchase, filling out a form, or signing up for a newsletter. Conversions are a crucial metric for measuring the effectiveness of an ad campaign, as they directly impact the advertiser's bottom line.

To track conversions, advertisers typically use conversion tracking tools, such as Google Analytics or Facebook Pixel. These tools allow advertisers to see which ads and channels are driving the most conversions and optimize their campaigns accordingly.

REMARKETING

Remarketing, also known as retargeting, is a powerful online marketing technique that allows advertisers to reach users who have previously interacted with their website or ads. By placing a cookie on a user's browser, advertisers can display targeted ads to these users as they browse other websites.

Remarketing is effective because it targets users who have already shown an interest in the advertiser's products or services. This can lead to higher conversion rates and better return on investment (ROI) compared to other forms of online advertising.

CLICK-THROUGH RATE (CTR)

Click-Through Rate (CTR) is a metric that measures the percentage of users who click on an ad after seeing it. CTR is calculated by dividing the number of clicks an ad receives by the number of impressions it generates.

CTR is an important metric for evaluating the effectiveness of an ad campaign, as it indicates how well the ad is resonating with the target audience. A high CTR suggests that the ad is relevant and compelling, while a low CTR may indicate that the ad needs to be optimized or that the targeting is off.

Let's walk through an example of how to calculate conversions for an online advertising campaign.

Suppose you run an e-commerce store selling handmade jewelry. You decide to run a Facebook ad campaign to drive sales of your newest collection. Here are the details of your campaign:

- Ad impressions (number of times your ad was displayed): 100,000
- Ad clicks (number of times users clicked on your ad): 2,000
- Total sales generated from the ad campaign: $10,000
- Average order value: $50

To calculate the conversion rate for this campaign, you need to determine the number of conversions (sales) and divide it by the number of ad clicks.

Number of conversions = Total sales generated / Average order value
Number of conversions = $10,000 / $50 = 200

Conversion rate = (Number of conversions / Ad clicks) * 100
Conversion rate = (200 / 2,000) * 100 = 10%

In this example, your Facebook ad campaign had a conversion rate of 10%, meaning that 10% of the users who clicked on your ad ended up making a purchase.

You can also calculate the cost per conversion, which is the amount you spent on the ad campaign divided by the number of conversions.

Cost per conversion = Ad spend / Number of conversions

Let's say you spent $500 on this Facebook ad campaign.

Cost per conversion = $500 / 200 = $2.50

This means that, on average, you spent $2.50 for each conversion generated from the ad campaign.

Additionally, you can calculate the click-through rate (CTR) for the ad campaign, which is the number of ad clicks divided by the number of ad impressions.

CTR = (Ad clicks / Ad impressions) * 100
CTR = (2,000 / 100,000) * 100 = 2%

In this example, your ad campaign had a click-through rate of 2%, meaning that 2% of the users who saw your ad clicked on it.

These metrics help you evaluate the performance of your online advertising campaign and make data-driven decisions to optimize your ad spend and improve your conversion rates.

SEARCH ENGINE MARKETING (SEM)

Search Engine Marketing (SEM) is a form of online marketing that involves promoting websites by increasing their visibility in search engine results pages (SERPs). SEM encompasses both paid advertising, such as Google Ads, and organic search engine optimization (SEO) techniques.

Paid search advertising allows advertisers to place ads on search engine results pages when users search for specific keywords. Advertisers bid on these keywords and pay each time a user clicks on their ad. This can be an effective way to drive targeted traffic to a website and generate conversions.

Organic SEO, on the other hand, involves optimizing a website's content and structure to improve its ranking in search engine results pages for relevant keywords. This can be achieved through various techniques, such as keyword research, on-page optimization, and link building.

SOCIAL MEDIA MARKETING

Social Media Marketing involves promoting a brand, product, or service through social media platforms, such as Facebook, Twitter, Instagram, and LinkedIn. Social media marketing can take many forms, including organic posts, paid advertising, influencer marketing, and user-generated content.

The goal of social media marketing is to engage with the target audience, build brand awareness, and drive traffic and conversions. By creating compelling content and leveraging the targeting capabilities of social media platforms, advertisers can reach their desired audience and achieve their marketing objectives.

CONTENT MARKETING

Content Marketing is a strategic approach to creating and distributing valuable, relevant, and consistent content to attract and retain a clearly defined audience. The goal of content marketing is to drive profitable customer action by building trust and credibility with the target audience.

Content marketing can take many forms, such as blog posts, videos, infographics, eBooks, and whitepapers. By providing informative and engaging content, businesses can attract and nurture leads, establish thought leadership, and ultimately drive conversions.

EMAIL MARKETING

Email Marketing involves sending promotional or informational messages to a list of subscribers via email. Email marketing can be used to promote products or services, share news and updates, or nurture leads and customers.

To be effective, email marketing campaigns should be targeted, personalized, and provide value to the recipient. This can be achieved through segmentation, dynamic content, and automation. By sending relevant and engaging emails, businesses can build relationships with their audience and drive conversions.

AFFILIATE MARKETING

Affiliate Marketing is a performance-based marketing strategy where advertisers pay publishers (affiliates) a commission for each conversion or sale generated through their promotional efforts. Affiliates promote the advertiser's products or services through various channels, such as websites, blogs, or social media, and earn a percentage of the revenue generated from each sale.

Affiliate marketing can be an effective way for advertisers to expand their reach and drive sales while providing publishers with a way to monetize their audience and content.

VIDEO MARKETING

Video Marketing involves creating and distributing video content to promote a brand, product, or service. Video marketing can be used to educate, entertain, or inspire the target audience and can be distributed through various channels, such as YouTube, social media, or embedded on a website.

Video marketing can be an effective way to engage with the target audience, as videos are more likely to be watched and shared compared to other forms of content. By creating compelling and informative videos, businesses can increase brand awareness, drive traffic, and generate conversions.

Online marketing is a vast and ever-evolving field that encompasses a wide range of strategies and tactics. From banner ads and search engine marketing to social media and content marketing, businesses have a plethora of options for reaching and engaging their target audience online.

By understanding the key concepts and metrics, such as cost per click, impressions, conversions, and click-through rates, marketers can develop effective online marketing campaigns that drive results and achieve their business objectives. As the digital landscape continues to evolve, staying up-to-date with the latest trends and best practices in online marketing will be essential for success in the years to come.

Sample Test Questions

1) Which of the following is NOT one of the Four P's?

   A) Price
   B) Promotion
   C) Production
   D) Place
   E) None of the above

The correct answer is C:) Production. The Four P's are (1) Product (2) Place (3) Promotion and (4) Price.

2) Which of the following is NOT a type of segmentation?

   A) Geographic
   B) Sociographic
   C) Psychographic
   D) Demographic
   E) All of the above are types of segmentation

The correct answer is B:) Sociographic.

3) _____ refers to a company's employment of inputs, such as men, material and money, into the company's overall marketing process in order to generate sales.

   A) Marketing mix
   B) Marketing allocation
   C) Marketing response
   D) Marketing effort
   E) None of the above

The correct answer is D:) Marketing effort.

4) Which of the following BEST describes the meaning of elastic in marketing?

    A) A product which holds its shape well.
    B) A product which people will buy no matter what price it is.
    C) A product which people will not buy if it is too expensive.
    D) A product which starts out selling good, but the demand for it does not last.
    E) A product which does sell well at first, but demand for it grows.

The correct answer is C:) A product which people will not buy if it is too expensive. On the other hand, inelastic products are products which people will buy no matter what price they are.

5) _____ refers to a company's overall objectives, tactics, policies and guidelines that govern over a period of that company's marketing effort.

    A) Marketing mix
    B) Marketing allocation
    C) Marketing response
    D) Marketing strategy
    E) None of the above

The correct answer is D:) Marketing strategy.

6) Which of the following describes cognitive dissonance?

    A) Advertising which is designed to support one side of a controversial issue.
    B) Starting a genuine relationship with the client and listening to their needs and concerns.
    C) Seeking out new customers and convincing them to buy the product for the first time.
    D) When a person has second thoughts about whether they purchased the correct product.
    E) None of the above

The correct answer is D:) When a person has second thoughts about whether they purchased the correct product. This can occur because they later realize they didn't really want or need it, or because they see advertisements for a competitive product.

7) _____ is the most important task of the Marketing Department to find out the optimum setting for its Marketing Decision Variables.

   A) Marketing mix
   B) Marketing allocation
   C) Marketing response
   D) Marketing effort
   E) None of the above

The correct answer is A:) Marketing mix.

8) Which of the following describes a star product?

   A) High market growth and high relative market share
   B) High market growth and low relative market share
   C) Low market growth and high relative market share
   D) Low market growth and low relative market share
   E) None of the above

The correct answer is A:) High market growth and high relative market share. These are products that lead in their fast growing market, and generate a lot of revenue.

9) _____ is related to the pattern of sales to the marketing effort.

   A) Marketing mix
   B) Marketing allocation
   C) Marketing response
   D) Marketing strategy
   E) None of the above

The correct answer is C:) Marketing response.

10) If a product has a retail price $550, and the markup is 10%, what was the wholesale price?

   A) $50
   B) $450
   C) $500
   D) $540
   E) Cannot be determined without more information

The correct answer is C:) $500. 10% of $500 is $50. $500+$50= $550.

11) Which act is also known as the "Chain Store Act"?

   A) Sherman Antitrust Act
   B) Clayton Act
   C) Robinson-Patman Act
   D) Federal Trade Commission Act
   E) North American Free Trade Agreement

The correct answer is C:) Robinson-Patman Act. The act made price discrimination between wholesalers and retailers illegal.

12) If a product has a wholesale price of $30 and a markup of 200%, what is its retail price?

   A) $32
   B) $50
   C) $90
   D) $200
   E) $230

The correct answer is C:) $90. 30+200% = 30+30(2.00) = 30+60 = 90.

13) Kbrand corporation wants to markup their alarm clocks 30% above their cost of $15. What would be the cost to the consumer?

   A) $19.50
   B) $10
   C) $20
   D) $22.50
   E) None of the above

The correct answer is A:) $19.50.

14) Marketing based on brand loyalty would be considered what type of segmentation?

   A) Demographic
   B) Geographic
   C) Psychographic
   D) Behavioral
   E) None of the above

The correct answer is D:) Behavioral. Behavioral segmentation is based on people's attitude toward the product.

15) Which of the following does the S stand for in SWOT analysis?

   A) Strategy
   B) Strength
   C) Superior
   D) Status
   E) None of the above

The correct answer is B:) Strength.

16) A new law regulating the amount of toxic fumes a factory is allowed to produce would be considered what type of change?

   A) Social
   B) Economic
   C) Technological
   D) Political
   E) Legal

The correct answer is E:) Legal. Legal changes can affect how businesses are allowed to market and function.

17) Which of the following is the correct path of a product lifecycle?

   A) Introduction, growth, reinvention, decline
   B) Market demand, production, growth, decline
   C) Market demand, production, decline, reinvention
   D) Introduction, growth, maturity, decline
   E) None of the above

The correct answer is D:) Introduction, growth, maturity, decline. Although many companies at the decline period add new features or reinvent the product to gain more sales, this is considered a "re-start" of the product lifecycle.

18) A war in the Middle East causes gas prices to rise. This is what type of change?

   A) Social
   B) Economic
   C) Technological
   D) Political
   E) Legal

The correct answer is D:) Political. Political changes can affect international trade, and in this case that caused gas prices to rise.

19) Which of the following refers to the number of product lines offered?

   A) Width
   B) Depth
   C) Consistency
   D) Line
   E) None of the above

The correct answer is A:) Width. Width to the number of product lines offered. For example, Mitsubishi produces a range of products from air conditioners, machines, electric appliances, cars, etc.

20) Which of the following was the first act to work against monopolies?

   A) Sherman Antitrust Act
   B) Clayton Act
   C) Robinson-Patman Act
   D) Federal Trade Commission Act
   E) North American Free Trade Agreement

The correct answer is A:) Sherman Antitrust Act. The Sherman Antitrust Act was passed in 1890 and was the first act to work against monopolies (or trusts) and cartels.

21) Which of the following refers to how similarly related the offered product lines in end use, production and distribution?

   A) Width
   B) Depth
   C) Consistency
   D) Line
   E) None of the above

The correct answer is C:) Consistency.

22) Which is the following is NOT a market segmentation variable?

   A) Population
   B) Benefits sought
   C) Spending pattern
   D) Marketing
   E) None of the above

The correct answer is D:) Marketing. Market segmentation variables can include all demographics, age, race, occupation as well as things such as personality and lifestyle.

23) Which of the following refers to the average number of products offered within each product line?

   A) Width
   B) Depth
   C) Consistency
   D) Line
   E) None of the above

The correct answer is B:) Depth. This refers to the average number of products offered within each product line. For example, LG produces Air conditioning machines with different capacities - 0.5 ton, 1.0 ton, 1.5 tons, 2.0 ton, split AC, etc.

24) A company buys 10 new machines to make baseball hats and each costs $1,200. They must pay 20 cents for each hat they make. They sell their hats for $5 each. They only plan to make as many as they need to break even. How many must they make (assuming they sell all the hats they make)?

   A) 1500
   B) 2000
   C) 2500
   D) 3000
   E) 3500

The correct answer is C:) 2500. The equation would be $10(1,200) + .20x = 5x$.

25) Which of the following best describes tariffs?

   A) Taxes on goods imported from or exported to another country.
   B) Any tax which is instituted by a national government.
   C) A tax which applies only to products made in a certain country.
   D) A percentage of any sold product which must be paid to the government.
   E) Both A and C

The correct answer is A:) Taxes on goods imported from or exported to another country.

26) Which of the following is a heterogeneous product?

   A) Cars
   B) Bubble wrap
   C) Produce
   D) Nails
   E) None of the above

The correct answer is C:) Produce.

27) When existing products are marketed to new groups it is called

   A) Market segmentation
   B) Product quality
   C) Product differentiation
   D) Product diversification
   E) Market expansion

The correct answer is E:) Market expansion.

28) Which of the following best describes advocacy advertising?

   A) Advertising which is designed to support one side of a controversial issue.
   B) Starting a genuine relationship with the client and listening to their needs and concerns.
   C) Seeking out new customers and convincing them to buy the product for the first time.
   D) When a person has second thoughts about whether they purchased the correct product.
   E) None of the above

The correct answer is A:) Advertising which is designed to support one side of a controversial issue. Essentially, it is advertising a person's viewpoint and they are trying to persuade others of their position.

29) This area is reviewed before introduction of a product into market and is completed by the engineering department.

   A) Market segmentation
   B) Product quality
   C) Product differentiation
   D) Product diversification
   E) Market expansion

The correct answer is B:) Product quality. Product quality should be reviewed and completed well before a product hits the market.

30) What does a marketing department do to show the benefits of a new product compared to other existing products?

   A) Market segmentation
   B) Product quality
   C) Product differentiation
   D) Product diversification
   E) Market expansion

The correct answer is C:) Product differentiation.

31) A salesperson that closely manages the relationship between physician and pharmaceutical companies including placing orders, providing samples and visiting the physician is called what?

   A) Service salesperson
   B) Multi-level-marketing salesperson
   C) Missionary salesperson
   D) Direct salesperson
   E) None of the above

The correct answer is C:) Missionary salesperson. Although the name is somewhat of a misnomer, a missionary salesperson closely manages the relationship between manufacturer and their customers.

32) This is done to increase product lines, avoiding seasonal fluctuations in demand and achieving a higher growth rate.

   A) Market segmentation
   B) Product quality
   C) Product differentiation
   D) Product diversification
   E) Market expansion

The correct answer is E:) Market expansion. Market expansion can increase product lines, insulate a company from relying financially on one product, avoid seasonal fluctuations by adding more products to the marketing mix and help achieve a higher growth rate.

33) Which of the following is most likely an inelastic product?

   A) Chocolate
   B) A new camera
   C) Going out to dinner
   D) Medicine
   E) All of the above are elastic

The correct answer is D:) Medicine. Whether or not it is expensive, people are likely to buy the medicine that they need. On the other hand, chocolate, a new camera and going out to dinner are all luxury activities that people generally do only if it is convenient and they can afford to do it.

34) An aftermarket car parts manufacturer sells their product to a distributor who then sells directly to retail car accessory stores. The manufacturer sells their product for $50 to the distributor who marks up the product 25% before selling to the retailer. The retailer then has a 100% markup on the product sold to the ultimate consumer. What is the price a retail customer will pay?

   A) $125
   B) $150
   C) $175
   D) $200
   E) $225

The correct answer is A:) $125. The initial price is $50. The markup the distributor adds is $12.50, making the product cost $62.50 to the retailer. Their markup is 100% of the product cost, or $62.50. $62.50 for the product plus $62.50 for the markup makes this item $125 for the ultimate consumer.

35) A grouping of consumers with similar needs and wants is called:

   A) Market segmentation
   B) Product quality
   C) Product differentiation
   D) Product diversification
   E) Market expansion

The correct answer is A:) Market segmentation. Any subset or a number of such subsets may be taken in as a target audience in that market and approached with a specific marketing mix. This is called market segmentation.

36) Which of the following is a tactic of push marketing?

   A) Customer relationship management
   B) Mass media promotion
   C) Point of sale displays
   D) Word of mouth
   E) Promotional discounts

The correct answer is C:) Point of sale displays. In push marketing, the customer encounters a product in a retail setting and is directly influenced to buy it.

37) Which of the following describes a problem child product?

   A) High market growth and high relative market share
   B) High market growth and low relative market share
   C) Low market growth and high relative market share
   D) Low market growth and low relative market share
   E) None of the above

The correct answer is B:) High market growth and low relative market share. They are called problem children because the market is growing fast and they have a lot of potential to do well, but the low relative market share means that they could fall into the dog category if or when the market slows down.

38) Clothing is considered

   A) Hard goods
   B) Electronics
   C) Soft goods
   D) Non-durable goods
   E) None of the above

The correct answer is C:) Soft goods. Textiles of any kind are referred to as soft goods.

39) Which type of product does a company NOT want to have?

   A) Cash cow
   B) Star
   C) Dog
   D) Problem child
   E) Question mark

The correct answer is C:) Dog. It may break even as far as costs go, but it doesn't have any real potential and ties up a lot of resources for a company. Financially speaking they are worthless assets.

40) Janipo Corporation owns three different apparel companies. One company is targeted to infants, one to plus size women and one to tweens. This is an example of

   A) Public relations
   B) Direct marketing
   C) Multi-level-marketing
   D) Differentiated marketing
   E) Customized marketing

The correct answer is D:) Differentiated marketing. In differentiated marketing, subgroups such as (1) Men (2) Women (3) Children (4) Youth, and (5) Elderly are created and the company offers differentiated products to suit the individual consumer of each such sub group.

41) Which of the following is an example of direct advertising?

- A) Internet ads
- B) Newspaper ads
- C) TV commercial
- D) Telemarketing
- E) All of the above

The correct answer is E:) All of the above. All of the methods listed are direct attempts by the company to promote their product.

42) An air conditioner is a type of

- A) Hard goods
- B) Electronics
- C) Soft goods
- D) Durable goods
- E) None of the above

The correct answer is D:) Durable goods. These tangible goods (actual goods), once bought, will satisfy for many years and include items such as air conditioners, appliances, etc.

43) If the economy falls into a sudden recession it would be considered what type of change?

- A) Social
- B) Economic
- C) Technological
- D) Political
- E) Legal

The correct answer is B:) Economic. Changes in inflation, interest rates and average wages are also economic changes.

44) Once the first level of Maslow's Hierarchy of Needs is met, consumers would be focused on which of the following?

   A) Housing in a safe area
   B) Groceries
   C) Products related to self-esteem
   D) Church tithes
   E) Charity

The correct answer is C:) Products related to self-esteem. The first level deals with the primary needs of a person such as food, water, shelter, etc. Once that need is met, the second level is presented which deals with self-esteem.

45) A person has a disposable income of $700 and a discretionary income of $300. What are their cost of living expenses?

   A) $300
   B) $400
   C) $500
   D) $700
   E) $1,000

The correct answer is B:) $400. Discretionary income is the leftover income after cost of living. Therefore, cost of living must be $700-$300 or $400.

46) Christy's Blinds wants to advertise in the local direct mail magazine. The cost is $1400 for 10,000 homes. Instead of paying the direct mail magazine in cash, the company trades blinds for the advertising space. This is called

   A) Public relations
   B) Importing
   C) Good business practice
   D) Barter
   E) Exporting

The correct answer is D:) Barter. Exchanging product, service or merchandise for anything other than cash is called bartering.

47) According to the Ansoff Matrix, _____ carries the highest risk, and _____ has the lowest potential risk.

   A) Diversification, market penetration
   B) Market penetration, product development
   C) Market development, diversification
   D) Diversification, product development
   E) Product development, market penetration

The correct answer is A:) Diversification, market penetration. The Ansoff Matrix illustrates a company's market growth opportunity.

48) This step in the sales process identifies potential customers

   A) Presenting
   B) Researching
   C) Prospecting
   D) Segmenting
   E) None of the above

The correct answer is C:) Prospecting.

49) If a business buys a new machine for 4,000 and each unit they produce costs them 5 cents, what must they charge for each unit to break even if they make and sell 500 units? Choose closest answer.

   A) $2
   B) $5
   C) $9
   D) $12
   E) $20

The correct answer is C:) $9. The equation would be 4,000+.05(500) = x (500), where x is the price.

50) A commission paid to a sales person, sometimes referred to as a "spiff" is also called what?

   A) Hush money
   B) Collateral
   C) Advances
   D) Push money
   E) None of the above

The correct answer is D:) Push money.

51) Which of the following is most likely a consumer product?

   A) Computer
   B) Iron
   C) Machines
   D) Steel
   E) All of the above are industrial goods

The correct answer is A:) Computer. Of the products listed, computers are the most likely to be bought for private use.

52) What is the average response rate for direct mail marketing?

   A) 2.6%
   B) 2%
   C) 10%
   D) 8%
   E) 4.1%

The correct answer is A:) 2.6%. Typically, a response rate of 2-3% is considered a successful campaign. However, those numbers can fluctuate on the industry and when considering justification, the cost of the mailing should be a consideration.

53) Which of the following eliminated tariffs between trade through Canada, the United States and Mexico?

   A) Sherman Antitrust Act
   B) Clayton Act
   C) Robinson-Patman Act
   D) Federal Trade Commission Act
   E) North American Free Trade Agreement

The correct answer is E:) North American Free Trade Agreement.

54) Producing a product for use in another country is called

   A) Exporting
   B) Wholesaling
   C) Franchising
   D) Licensing
   E) Importing

The correct answer is A:) Exporting.

55) Which of the following would NOT be considered a tariff?

   A) A government tax on oil imported from Saudi Arabia to the United States.
   B) A tax on toys being outsourced to China, and then shipped back to the United States.
   C) A sales tax on oranges grown in California and shipped to stores in Maine.
   D) A tax on German chocolate imported to the United States.
   E) All of the above are considered tariffs.

The correct answer is C:) A sales tax on oranges grown in California and shipped to stores in Maine. Tariffs apply when products are imported from or exported to another country. California and Maine are both in the United States.

56) Disney Corporation gives ABC corporation permission to put Mickey Mouse on their lunch boxes for a fee. What is this called?

   A) Exporting
   B) Wholesaling
   C) Franchising
   D) Licensing
   E) Importing

The correct answer is D:) Licensing.

57) Which type of product does a company most want to have?

   A) Cash cow
   B) Star
   C) Dog
   D) Problem child
   E) Question mark

The correct answer is A:) Cash cow. This is the best type of product to have because it allows the company to make a lot of money, with little investment needed.

58) The stages in the life cycle of a product are introduction, growth, maturity, and decline. During which phase of the product life cycle does product have its highest sales?

   A) Introduction
   B) Growth
   C) Maturity
   D) Decline
   E) Sales are equal through all four stages

The correct answer is C:) Maturity. The maturity stage is often considered the most competitive. During this stage, new competitors begin filling in the market and the growth rate of market sales declines.

59) What is the difference between disposable and discretionary income?

   A) Discretionary income is income before taxes are removed. Disposable income is income after taxes are removed.
   B) Disposable income is income after taxes are removed. Discretionary income is income after taxes are removed and all bills and living expenses are paid.
   C) Disposable income is income that a household spends maintaining their standard of living. Discretionary income is income that is saved or invested.
   D) Discretionary income is the income spent on bills and living expenses. Disposable income is income that is saved or invested.
   E) There is no difference; they are two terms with the same meaning.

The correct answer is B:) Disposable income is income after taxes are removed. Discretionary income is income after taxes are removed and all bills and living expenses are paid. Disposable income and discretionary income are characterized by the difference between needs and wants.

60) The process of bringing in goods from a foreign country for the purpose of selling them is called what?

   A) Exporting
   B) Wholesaling
   C) Franchising
   D) Licensing
   E) Importing

The correct answer is E:) Importing.

61) In 1794, the invention of the cotton gin changed the South by making it far more profitable to mass produce cotton. This change is considered to have been

A) Social
B) Economic
C) Technological
D) Political
E) Legal

The correct answer is C:) Technological. Technology affects all levels of marketing. This makes keeping up with the changes an important element of marketing.

62) Purchasing from the manufacturer and reselling to the retailer is called what?

A) Exporting
B) Wholesaling
C) Franchising
D) Licensing
E) Importing

The correct answer is B:) Wholesaling.

63) Which of the following was passed as an amendment to the Sherman Antitrust Act to clarify it?

A) Sherman Antitrust Act
B) Clayton Act
C) Robinson-Patman Act
D) Federal Trade Commission Act
E) North American Free Trade Agreement

The correct answer is B:) Clayton Act.

64) Which of the following would NOT be a SMART objective?

A) To reduce costs in production 5% by January 2015
B) To increase sales by 10% in Q3
C) To hire three researchers by the end of next month
D) To open two new locations
E) To gain 15% of the market share by March 2010

The correct answer is D:) To open two new locations. This item is not specific enough, nor timed so it would NOT be considered a SMART objective.

65) A paper company has been selling paper to an office building for over 20 years. Their selling style would be best classified as

   A) Relationship
   B) Technological
   C) Demographical
   D) Missionary
   E) None of the above

The correct answer is A:) Relationship. Relationship selling follows the theory that it is easier to maintain a client than to find a new one.

66) The O in SWOT analysis stands for what?

   A) Online
   B) Organization
   C) Ornamentation
   D) Opportunities
   E) None of the above

The correct answer is D:) Opportunities.

67) Which of the following is a homogeneous product?

   A) Produce
   B) Donuts
   C) Nails
   D) Custom clothing
   E) None of the above

The correct answer is C:) Nails.

68) When you can only buy the latest video game from Walmart, the manufacturer for that game is participating in

   A) Incentive distribution
   B) Geographic distribution
   C) Exclusive distribution
   D) Determined distribution
   E) None of the above

The correct answer is C:) Exclusive distribution. Exclusive distribution is when a company determines one retailer per country, state or city will be the only way of purchasing their product.

69) Which of the following products is most likely elastic?

   A) Medicine
   B) Candy
   C) Gas
   D) Water
   E) All of the above are inelastic

The correct answer is B:) Candy. Of the items on the list, candy is the one that a person is least likely to buy if it is too expensive.

70) What is the first step in the process of decision making of a purchase?

   A) Shopping around
   B) Recommendations
   C) Purchase evaluation
   D) Research
   E) Need awareness

The correct answer is E:) Need awareness.

71) If a product has a wholesale price of $750 and the retail price is $1,000, what is the markup percentage?

   A) 20%
   B) 33%
   C) 50%
   D) 75%
   E) 100%

The correct answer is B:) 33%. The difference between the two is $250, which is 33% of $750.

72) Which of the following is NOT a part of the Promotion marketing mix?

   A) Advertising
   B) Personal selling
   C) Sales promotion
   D) Publicity
   E) None of the above

The correct answer is E:) None of the above. Advertising, personal selling, sales promotion, and publicity are the four parts of the promotion marketing mix.

73) Marketing geared toward people with similar interests would be considered

   A) Demographic segmentation
   B) Geographic segmentation
   C) Psychographic segmentation
   D) Behavioral segmentation
   E) None of the above

The correct answer is C:) Psychographic segmentation. Psychographic segments are segments with similar lifestyles. These are groups of people with similar activities, values, interests, personalities and opinions.

74) When a company compares their performance to another's it is called

   A) Benchmarking
   B) Competitive advantage
   C) Diversification
   D) Differentiation
   E) Market share report

The correct answer is A:) Benchmarking. Benchmarking is the process of comparing a company's performance to that of another company, sometimes in the same industry or sector.

75) Which of the following presidents became known as a "trustbuster" for his use of the Sherman Antitrust Act?

   A) Harry Truman
   B) Theodore Roosevelt
   C) William Howard Taft
   D) Franklin D Roosevelt
   E) Grover Cleveland

The correct answer is B:) Theodore Roosevelt. Although the act was passed nearly ten years before his presidency, Roosevelt was the first to really use it to work against monopolies.

76) Which of the following is not a part of the SMART approach to creating objectives?

   A) Specific
   B) Measurable
   C) Achievable
   D) Realistic
   E) None of the above

The correct answer is E:) None of the above. The acronym SMART is used to create objectives that will be of the most benefit to the company. SMART stands for Specific, Measurable, Achievable, Realistic, and Timed.

77) The selling style of door to door salesmen is best classified as

   A) Relationship
   B) Technological
   C) Demographical
   D) Missionary
   E) None of the above

The correct answer is D:) Missionary. Missionary selling involves seeking out new customers and convincing them to buy the product for the first time.

78) A company that specializes in Halloween costumes and merchandise would have what type of a sales cycle?

   A) Upward moving trend
   B) Seasonal
   C) Flat line
   D) Stagnant
   E) None of the above

The correct answer is B:) Seasonal. Seasonal or cyclical sales patterns are typically regular and easy to predict.

79) Cognitive dissonance is also called

    A) Advocacy advertising
    B) Disposable income
    C) Buyer's remorse
    D) Inelastic demand
    E) Either A or C

The correct answer is C:) Buyer's remorse.

80) Which of the following is NOT a part of AOSTC?

    A) Analysis
    B) Objectives
    C) Strategies
    D) Tests
    E) Controls

The correct answer is D:) Tests.

81) Which of the following is an example of indirect advertising?

    A) Newspaper ads
    B) Internet ads
    C) TV commercials
    D) Word of mouth advertising
    E) Both B and D

The correct answer is D:) Word of mouth advertising. Word of mouth advertising isn't a direct advertisement of the company so it is indirect advertising.

82) The T is SWOT analysis stands for what?

    A) Testimonials
    B) Threats
    C) Territory
    D) Transformation
    E) None of the above

The correct answer is B:) Threats.

83) A college student working a part-time job makes $800 a month after taxes. They have to pay $300 on their dorm (which includes utilities) and they have a meal plan that costs $130 a month. Their tuition has been broken down into monthly payments of $250. They have set aside $20 a month to go to the movies. What is their discretionary income?

   A) $800
   B) $500
   C) $120
   D) $100
   E) Cannot be determined without more information

The correct answer is C:) $120. There are no savings mentioned and cost of living includes the dorm costs, meal plan and tuition because these are the costs the student must pay. The movies fall under discretionary income and don't need to be considered in the calculations.

84) Because buyer's attitudes do not change very quickly, which of the following would be the best way to increase product awareness of a low fat butter?

   A) Grocery store demonstrations
   B) Coupons in the newspaper
   C) Television advertising
   D) Product placement
   E) All of the above

The correct answer is E:) All of the above. The more experienced a customer is with a name or a brand, the more likely they are to try it or buy it.

85) Which of the following is most likely an industrial product?

   A) Sports cars
   B) Board games
   C) Sugar
   D) Steel
   E) All of the above are consumer goods

The correct answer is D:) Steel. Of the items listed, steel is the least likely to be bought for personal use and the most likely to be bought for the manufacture of other items.

86) When a mixer is sold a three different major retail chains but each store has the identical pricing, it is easy to assume that the product is _____ by the manufacturer.

   A) Price fixing
   B) Price controlled
   C) Price differentiation
   D) Price discrimination
   E) None of the above

The correct answer is B:) Price controlled. Many products have a suggested MSRP (manufacturer's suggested retail price) while others have a MAP (minimum advertised price). MSRP is a suggestion while MAP is many times tied to a contract. Game system manufacturer's and audio electronics companies are a great example of MAP.

87) Which of the following BEST describes a cash cow product?

   A) High market growth and high relative market share
   B) High market growth and low relative market share
   C) Low market growth and high relative market share
   D) Low market growth and low relative market share
   E) None of the above

The correct answer is C:) Low market growth and high relative market share. In other words, it is one of the most recognized products in a field that doesn't sustain much change.

88) The CEO of a major corporation giving a talk show interview is an example of

   A) Advertising
   B) Goodwill
   C) Public relations
   D) Revenue generating
   E) None of the above

The correct answer is C:) Public relations.

89) If a product has a markup of $50 and the wholesale price is $100. What is the markup percentage?

   A) 10%
   B) 40%
   C) 50%
   D) 60%
   E) 70%

The correct answer is C:) 50%. 50 is 50% of 100.

90) Handling objections is part of

   A) Personal selling
   B) Advertising
   C) Marketing mix
   D) The four p's
   E) AOSTC

The correct answer is A:) Personal selling. Personal selling uses a five step process. It begins when a sales person (1) identifies a lead by prospecting, (2) makes a call or sends a letter to their prospect, (3) makes sales call/presentation, (4) handles any objectives by the customer and then (5) closes the sale. Personal selling is used in areas where the product is expensive, complicated or the price is negotiable. Examples include office copying systems, some insurance plans, high-end medical instruments, etc.

91) Which of the following is NOT true of the Federal Trade Commission Act?

   A) It created the Federal Trade Commission.
   B) It prevents unfair business practices.
   C) It gives the government the right to issue cease and desist orders.
   D) It prevents deceptive business practices.
   E) It made illegal any contract, deal, conspiracy or scheme to restrain trade.

The correct answer is E:) It made illegal any contract, deal, conspiracy or scheme to restrain trade. This was done by the Sherman Antitrust Act.

92) Which of the following is NOT a marketing control?

   A) Sales channel
   B) Market analysis
   C) Budgeting
   D) Cash flow statements
   E) Market research

The correct answer is A:) Sales channel. Market analysis, budgeting, cash flow statements and market research are all a part of marketing control.

93) Which of the following describes a dog product?

   A) High market growth and high relative market share
   B) High market growth and low relative market share
   C) Low market growth and high relative market share
   D) Low market growth and low relative market share
   E) None of the above

The correct answer is D:) Low market growth and low relative market share. It is a product in a slowly growing industry with little recognition. Financially speaking, they are worthless assets.

94) A decline in purchasing power due to price levels rising faster than income is called

   A) Price elasticity
   B) Balance of trade
   C) Market share penetration
   D) Inflation
   E) None of the above

The correct answer is D:) Inflation.

95) Which of the following acts amended the Clayton Act?

   A) Sherman Antitrust Act
   B) Clayton Act
   C) Robinson-Patman Act
   D) Federal Trade Commission Act
   E) North American Free Trade Agreement

The correct answer is C:) Robinson-Patman Act. The act expanded the Clayton Act to include not only local price cuts, but other forms of price discrimination as well.

96) Typically, who is the dominant member of the household responsible for selecting food items?

   A) Husband
   B) Wife
   C) Children
   D) Both husband and wife
   E) The entire family

The correct answer is B:) Wife. Typically, the wife is responsible for selecting food items, kitchenware, kitchen appliances, etc.

97) Which of the following acts gave the government the authority to issue cease and desist orders to companies using unfair or deceptive business practices?

   A) Sherman Antitrust Act
   B) Clayton Act
   C) Robinson-Patman Act
   D) Federal Trade Commission Act
   E) North American Free Trade Agreement

The correct answer is D:) Federal Trade Commission Act. The act was designed to prevent deceptive and unfair business practices and the FTC was created to do that.

98) Which of the following BEST describes push strategy promotion?

   A) Bringing the product to the consumer.
   B) Bringing the consumer to the product.
   C) Creating a demand for the product so that the consumer will seek it through their local stores.
   D) Pushing the product over so that someone will pick it up and possibly buy it.
   E) Both A and C

The correct answer is A:) Bringing the product to the consumer. The idea of push strategy is essentially putting the product somewhere that people are most likely to become aware of it and immediately buy it. Answers B and C describe pull strategy.

99) Segmentation based on gender would be classified as

   A) Demographic
   B) Geographic
   C) Psychographic
   D) Behavioral
   E) None of the above

The correct answer is A:) Demographic. Demographic segments are related to classifications of people within a population. This includes people with similar age, family situation, ethnicity, gender, jobs, income or religion.

100) A change in the average age of a population would be considered what type of change?

   A) Social
   B) Economic
   C) Technological
   D) Political
   E) Legal

The correct answer is A:) Social. Social changes are changes which relate to behavior and lifestyle.

101) Which of the following is NOT true of NAFTA?

   A) NAFTA stands for North American Free Trade Agreement.
   B) As a part of NAFTA, Canada and the United States agree to help Mexico in trade matters.
   C) NAFTA works to lower trade barriers between the United States, Canada and Mexico.
   D) NAFTA is responsible for dealing with trade disputes between the United States, Canada and Mexico.
   E) None of the above

The correct answer is B:) As a part of NAFTA, Canada and the United States agree to help Mexico in trade matters. Answers A, C and D all describe responsibilities of NAFTA.

102) The wheel of retailing refers to the _____ of a company.

   A) Progression
   B) Economics
   C) Marketing strategy
   D) Sales
   E) Accounting

The correct answer is A:) Progression.

103) Which of the following e-commerce models describes when consumers post offers for goods or services online and business decide whether they wish to sell at the specified price?

   A) C2C
   B) B2C
   C) C2B
   D) B2B
   E) None of the above

The correct answer is C:) C2B. This is also called the consumer to business model.

104) A billboard is an example of

   A) Active listening
   B) Two-way communication
   C) One-way communication
   D) Psychographic
   E) None of the above

The correct answer is C:) One-way communication.

105) E-commerce is

   A) The buying and selling of goods and services over the internet.
   B) Conducting of business over the internet.
   C) The term used to describe online auction sites.
   D) Selling via an MLM system.
   E) None of the above

The correct answer is A:) The buying and selling of goods and services over the internet. E-commerce can consist of multiple different combinations of interactions between businesses and consumers.

106) John is paid $1500 per computer he sells. This is his only compensation. This means he

   A) Is paid salary
   B) Is paid on commission
   C) Is paid piecework
   D) Is paid both salary and commission
   E) None of the above

The correct answer is B:) Is paid on commission. When a person is only paid a percentage or fixed amount based on the amount they sell, it is called commission only.

107) Trade restrictions are a(n)

   A) Anomaly
   B) Embargo
   C) Reverse royalty
   D) Trade deficit
   E) None of the above

The correct answer is B:) Embargo. Embargoes can be limited to certain products or can be all inclusive and targeted at specific countries.

108) When the main actor in a television show drinks a certain kind of cola, that can be referred to as

   A) Marketing
   B) Product
   C) Promotion
   D) Product placement
   E) None of the above

The correct answer is D:) Product placement.

109) Which of the following BEST describes pull strategy promotion?

   A) Bringing the product to the consumer.
   B) Bringing the consumer to the product.
   C) Creating a demand for the product so that the consumer will seek it through their local stores.
   D) Pulling the product to the front of the store so consumers are more likely to be aware of it.
   E) Both B and C

The correct answer is E:) Both B and C. Pull strategy involves creating a demand for the product that will pull it through the stages, such as with a TV commercial. Answers A and D describe push strategy promotion.

110) Sending a customer a postcard in the mail detailing a website with special pricing is a form of

   A) Public relations
   B) Direct marketing
   C) Multi-level-marketing
   D) Differentiated marketing
   E) Customized marketing

The correct answer is B:) Direct marketing. If this marketing program had been only to a select demographic or target audience, it may have been considered customized marketing. However, since it was not, it falls under the category of direct marketing.

111) Which of the following was specifically mentioned in the Clayton Act?

   A) Conspiracies
   B) Schemes
   C) Strikes
   D) Boycotts
   E) Both C and D

The correct answer is E:) Both C and D. Strikes and boycotts were both legalized through the Clayton Act. However, conspiracies and schemes were mentioned in the Sherman Antitrust Act, not the Clayton Act.

112) John has an amazing restaurant. It is successfully, busy and unique. John decides that other people may want to open a restaurant just like his. By giving permission to copy the concept, help with recipes and consulting advice, Mary agrees to pay an up-front fee and a portion of her profits to John. What is this called?

A) Exporting
B) Wholesaling
C) Franchising
D) Licensing
E) Importing

The correct answer is C:) Franchising. The franchisee may also be required to sign a list of rules or other operating agreements to follow in addition to providing a royalty on all sales to the franchisor. Examples of franchises are McDonald's, Subway, and UPS store locations.

113) Segmentation based on what part of the country a person lives in would be classified as

A) Demographic
B) Geographic
C) Psychographic
D) Behavioral
E) None of the above

The correct answer is B:) Geographic. Geographic segmentation is segmentation based on location.

114) Antitrust laws are federal and state statutes that have been developed to protect _____ from unfair business practices such as monopolies and price fixing that could infringe on an open-market economy.

A) Consumers
B) Homebuyers
C) Truck drivers
D) Employees
E) None of the above

The correct answer is A:) Consumers. Antitrust laws such as the Sherman Act of 1890 were specifically introduced to prevent the formation of business monopolies and the restraint of free trade following the late 19th century surge in large conglomerates, especially in the railroad industry.

115) A marketing break-even point is calculated by taking _____ and dividing by the price minus the variable costs.

   A) Contribution margin
   B) Fixed costs
   C) Dependent costs
   D) Variable costs
   E) None of the above

The correct answer is B:) Fixed costs. The break-even point is the point at which company sales are exactly enough to cover its expenses.

116) The _____ formula equals gross profit divided by wholesale cost, and is used to determine the final selling price of an item.

   A) Markup
   B) Variable cost
   C) Fixed cost
   D) Contribution margin
   E) Profit margin

The correct answer is A:) Markup. By using the above formula, a seller can determine the amount they need to markup a product to determine the final selling price.

117) Marginal revenue is the amount gained by producing _____ additional unit(s) of a product or service.

   A) Five
   B) Two
   C) Ten
   D) One
   E) None of the above

The correct answer is D:) One. The purpose of marginal revenue is to determine the profitability of selling more products. By calculating the amount gained by adding one additional unit, a business can perform price comparisons to determine whether an increase in unit sales is needed.

118) Focus groups are a diverse group of individuals gathered together to provide feedback on products

   A) After they are launched to the public
   B) While they are being released to the public
   C) Before they are launched to the public
   D) That will never be released to the public
   E) None of the above

The correct answer is C:) Before they are launched to the public. The purpose of focus groups is to see the reactions of a smaller group of individuals to get an impression of how the larger public will react to a new product or service in time to make adjustments if necessary.

119) When a business wants to target as many consumers as possible with a product or message, they conduct _____, as opposed to niche marketing.

   A) Undifferentiated marketing
   B) Concentrated marketing
   C) Sales marketing
   D) Differentiated marketing
   E) None of the above

The correct answer is A:) Undifferentiated marketing. This type of marketing tends to be less expensive and reaches more consumers, versus niche or concentrated marketing, which focuses on one particular group of consumers. The downside of undifferentiated marketing is that you target such a diverse group that you cannot always predict how they will react to your product or service.

120) Product development is the plan that businesses use to improve an existing product or develop new products, while market penetration is the plan to _____ the market share of an existing market product or service.

   A) Decrease
   B) Increase
   C) Halve
   D) Quarter
   E) None of the above

The correct answer is B:) Increase. The purpose of market penetration is to increase sales through additional marketing or ramped up sale efforts in order to gain more of a particular market segment with an existing customer base.

121) If you have a selling price of $3.50 and a product cost of $2.79, your markup percentage is _____.

A) 40%
B) 45%
C) 25%
D) 35%
E) 30%

The correct answer is C:) 25%. Using the selling price minus the product cost to determine the gross profit of $0.71, you can then plug the gross profit number into the equation of markup equals gross profit divided by product cost to determine the markup, then multiply that number by 100 to find the markup percentage.

122) If you take in revenue of $400,000 on a product and the cost of goods sold is $200,000, then your gross profit is _____.

A) $200,000
B) $250,000
C) $125,000
D) $175,000
E) $100,000

The correct answer is A:) $200,000. To find the gross profit, you take the revenue received minus the cost of goods sold.

123) If you have a break-even point in units of 2,500, a variable cost per unit of $300, and a sale price per unit of $600, then your total fixed costs is _____.

A) $100,000
B) $350,000
C) $750,000
D) $600,000
E) $450,000

The correct answer is C:) $750,000. By using the formula break-even point in units equals total fixed costs divided by sale price per unit minus variable costs per unit, you can rearrange the equation to find the total fixed costs.

124) The Tariff Act of 1789 was also called the _____ Tariff.

   A) Washington
   B) McKinley
   C) Jefferson
   D) Hamilton
   E) Adams

The correct answer is D:) Hamilton. The Tariff Act of 1789 was the first of three tariffs conceived by Alexander Hamilton, the U.S. Secretary of the Treasury, who wanted to encourage the growth of U.S. manufacturing and remove the U.S. dependence on foreign imports.

125) The purpose of _____ is to solicit potential customers with which a business has not had prior contact.

   A) Product development
   B) Market penetration
   C) Product placement
   D) Direct marketing
   E) Cold calling

The correct answer is E:) Cold calling. Cold calling is typically done over the phone, but can also be done door-to-door with the express purpose of gaining additional profit through the increase in customer sales.

126) _____ is the practice of gaining exposure by featuring a specific product in a movie or television program.

   A) Product placement
   B) Product development
   C) Product management
   D) Product manipulation
   E) None of the above

The correct answer is A:) Product placement. Product management is the planning cycle associated with the production and selling of a product. Product development is the plan that businesses use to improve an existing product or develop new products. Product manipulation is a fabricated answer.

127) The theory of _____ refers to the belief that it exists when two or more conflicting attitudes exist by one individual about a product or service.

   A) Product development
   B) Product displacement
   C) Cognitive psychology
   D) Cognitive development
   E) Cognitive dissonance

The correct answer is E:) Cognitive dissonance. Cognitive dissonance usually occurs after a large purchase such as a car or house because people start to realize the significant commitment required to manage these large products.

128) The strategy for developing and marketing a product to a specific and well-defined market segment is called

   A) Product marketing
   B) Concentrated marketing
   C) Undifferentiated marketing
   D) Sales marketing
   E) None of the above

The correct answer is B:) Concentrated marketing. The goal behind concentrated marketing is that you are designing and manufacturing a product for a specific population within a market segment to better sell your product.

Test Taking Strategies

Here are some test-taking strategies that are specific to this test and to other CLEP tests in general:

- Keep your eyes on the time. Pay attention to how much time you have left.

- Read the entire question and read all the answers. Many questions are not as hard to answer as they may seem. Sometimes, a difficult sounding question really only is asking you how to read an accompanying chart. Chart and graph questions are on most CLEP tests and should be an easy free point.

- If you don't know the answer immediately, the new computer-based testing lets you mark questions and come back to them later if you have time.

- Read the wording carefully. Some words can give you hints to the right answer. There are no exceptions to an answer when there are words in the question such as always, all or none. If one of the answer choices includes most or some of the right answers, but not all, then that is not the correct answer. Here is an example:

    The primary colors include all of the following:

    A) Red, Yellow, Blue, Green

    B) Red, Green, Yellow

    C) Red, Orange, Yellow

    D) Red, Yellow, Blue

    E) None of the above

- Although item A includes all the right answers, it also includes an incorrect answer, making it incorrect. If you didn't read it carefully, were in a hurry, or didn't know the material well, you might fall for this.

- Make a guess on a question that you do not know the answer to. There is no penalty for an incorrect answer. Eliminate the answer choices that you know are incorrect. For example, this will let your guess be a 1 in 3 chance instead.

What Your Score Means

Based on your score, you may, or may not, qualify for credit at your specific institution. At University of Phoenix, a score of 50 is passing for full credit. At Utah Valley University, the score is unpublished, the school will accept credit on a case-by-case basis. Another school, Brigham Young University (BYU) does not accept CLEP credit. To find out what score you need for credit, you need to get that information from your school's website or academic advisor.

You can score between 20 and 80 on any CLEP test. Some exams include percentile ranks. Each correct answer is worth one point. You lose no points for unanswered or incorrect questions.

Test Preparation

How much you need to study depends on your knowledge of a subject area. If you are interested in literature, took it in school, or enjoy reading then your studying and preparation for the literature or humanities test will not need to be as intensive as someone who is new to literature.

This book is much different than the regular CLEP study guides. This book actually teaches you the information that you need to know to pass the test. If you are particularly interested in an area, or you want more information, do a quick search online. We've tried not to include too much depth in areas that are not as essential on the test. Everything in this book will be on the test. It is important to understand all major theories and concepts listed in the table of contents. It is also very important to know any bolded words.

Don't worry if you do not understand or know a lot about the area. With minimal study, you can complete and pass the test.

One of the fallacies of other test books is test questions. People assume that the **content** of the questions are similar to what will be on the test. **That is not the case.** They are only to test your "test taking skills" so for those who know to read a question carefully, there is not much added value from taking a "fake" test.

To prepare for the test, make a series of goals. Allot a certain amount of time to review the information you have already studied and to learn additional material. Take notes as you study, as it will help you learn the material.

Legal Note

All rights reserved. This Study Guide, Book and Flashcards are protected under US Copyright Law. No part of this book or study guide or flashcards may be reproduced, distributed or stored in a retrieval system, or transmitted in any form or by any means, electronic, mechanical, photocopying, recording, or otherwise, without the prior written permission of the publisher Breely Crush Publishing, LLC. This manual is not supported by or affiliated with the College Board, creators of the CLEP test. CLEP is

a registered trademark of the College Entrance Examination Board, which does not endorse this book.

References

[1] *Adapted from Richard P. Coleman "The continuing significance of social class to marketing." "Journal of Consumer Research, December 1983, pp.265-80."*

[2] *Source: William D. Wells & George Gubar. "Life Cycle Concepts in Marketing Research," Journal of Marketing Research, Nov. 1996, pp. 355-63)*

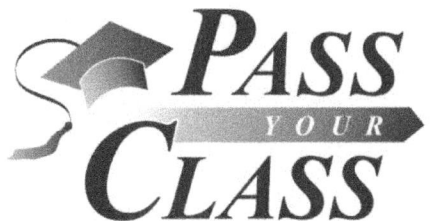

FLASHCARDS

This section contains flashcards for you to use to further your understanding of the material and test yourself on important concepts, names or dates. Read the term or question then flip the page over to check the answer on the back. Keep in mind that this information may not be covered in the text of the study guide. Take your time to study the flashcards, you will need to know and understand these concepts to pass the test.

Demand	What are the four P's?
Marketing Mix	Four Macro Economic Factors
Disposable Income	Components of Product Mix
Components of Price Mix	Components of Place Mix

Product, Price, Place Promotion	The need or want for a certain product
(1) Prosperity (also known as boom). (2) Recession (it is a slow down of business). (3) Depression (gloom also called bust stage), and (4) Recovery (the economic upswing).	A company's products and promotions
Product line, quality, packaging, branding	Income that is earned but not set aside for a specific need - spending money
Logistics, sales territories, types of channels, market location	Basic price, transport, credit terms

Components of Promotion Mix	**Durable Goods**
Non-durable Goods	**Services**
Convenient Goods	**Shopping Goods**
Specialty Goods	**Self-actualization**

These tangible goods (actual goods), which once bought will satisfy you for many years. (Example: Air Conditioners, Refrigerators, Clothing, etc).	Advertising, Publicity, Personal Selling, Sales Promotion
These non-tangible activities, benefits and satisfactions that are offered by individuals with expertise. (Example: Tailoring, Hair dressing, Cleaning, General Repairing etc).	These are also tangible goods which once bought may be consumed in a very short period of time. (Example: Toothpaste, Soap, Ham, biscuits, etc).
Goods bought by consumers after spending time on its utility, value, quality, suitability, style and of course, price. (Example: Cars, Home appliances. Dress materials, Furniture, etc).	Goods bought by consumers most often with relative speed without spending time on comparison. (Example: Newspapers, soaps, detergents, tobacco products, etc).
Highest need in Maslow's hierarchy of needs - Level 5	Goods bought by consumers that have characteristics perceived to be unique and/or having good brand identification. (Example: Branded goods, fancy goods, electronic goods, photographic equipment etc).

Esteem Needs	**Belonging and Love**
Safety	**Physical Needs**
Caste	**Social Class**
Reference Groups	**Face to Face Groups**

Level 3 need	Level 4 need
Level 1 need	Level 2 need
Identifies members on the basis of (superior or inferior) positions held by them	Aspirations of members is largely in keeping with the known and traditionally followed systems and practices
These are groups which have direct and immediate influence on a person's opinions, likes and dislikes. Example: The person's family, friends, neighbors, peers etc.	A person may not be a member of such groups but identifies with it and aspires to become one - such groups are known as reference groups

Family	Biogenic Needs
Psychogenic Needs	Examples of Demographic Segmentation
Extended Product	Four Stages of the Product Lifecycle
Sales Channel	In the four P's, what is place referred to?

Concerned with your physiological state. Example: Hunger, thirst, discomfort, etc.	A persons basic attitudes, behaviors and beliefs are during the formative years, formed through interaction with his family, which plays a most enduring role in such attitude formation
Sex, age, status	A persons specific need satisfaction relating to his psychological state of mind, which normally is not apparent. Example: Satisfying need for recognition, esteem, etc.
Introduction, Growth, Maturity, Decline	Tangible products - together with a gamut of service going with the products
How or where customers get your product	Through who a good is sold until it reaches the consumer

Federal Trade Commission	**Cartel**
Direct marketing	**Indirect marketing**
Star	**Cash cow**
Problem child	**Dog**

A group of distinct firms that work together essentially creating a monopoly.	A five person, bipartisan board created by the Federal Trade Commission Act.
A more neutral approach to advertising which includes word of mouth advertising or recognition through participation in the community.	A hands on approach to marketing which includes telemarketing and advertisements.
A product with a high market share in a slow growing industry.	A product with a high market share in a fast growing industry.
A product with low market growth and low relative market share.	A product with a low relative market share in a fast growing market.

| Advocacy advertising | Clayton Act |

| Question mark | Buyer's remorse |

| Pull promotion | Push promotion |

| Legal changes | Economic changes |

Amendment to Sherman Antitrust Act which specifically mentioned local price cuts and exclusive sales contracts.	Advertising which is designed to support one side of a controversial issue.
Another name for cognitive dissonance.	Another name for a problem child.
Bringing the product to the consumer and making sure they know about it.	Bringing the consumer to the product and creating a demand for it.
Changes in the state of the economy, inflation, interest rates and average wages are also economic changes.	Changes in laws which affect how business function.

Political changes	Social changes
Discretionary income	Heterogeneous
Robinson-Patman Act	Psychographic segments
Technological changes	Inelastic demand

Changes which relate to behavior and lifestyle.	Changes on a worldwide level which effect trade.
Diverse or varied products.	Discretionary income is income that is left over after a person has paid for basic necessities.
Groups of people with similar activities, values, interests, personalities and opinions.	Expanded Clayton Act to include all forms of price discrimination.
Inelastic products are products that people will buy no matter what the cost.	Increases and advancements in technology which change how people consider the market.

Missionary selling	Sherman Antitrust Act
Homogeneous	Market growth rate
Markup	Industrial Products
Disposable income	NAFTA

Made it illegal for any contract, deal, conspiracy or scheme to restrain trade.	Involves seeking out new customers and convincing them to buy the product for the first time.
Market growth rate is how quickly the particular market is growing for a product.	Manufactured to be all the same.
Meant to be bought by companies and used to produce other products.	Markup is the difference between the actual price of the product to the store and the price they sell the product for.
North American Free Trade Agreement. Established free trade among Canada, the United States and Mexico.	Net income after taxes.

Monopoly	**Demographic segments**
Federal Trade Commission Act	**Elastic demand**
Relative market share	**Geographic segments**
Behavioral segments	**Tariff**

People with similar age, family situation, ethnicity, gender, jobs, income, religion.	One company is the sole manufacturer of a product and there is no close substitute.
Products for which the demand varies greatly dependent on price.	Prevents companies from using unfair or deceptive business practices.
Segmentation based on location.	Relative market share is how prominent the product is within the market.
Tariffs are taxes levied on goods imported from (or exported to) another country.	Segmentation based on people's attitude toward the product.

Relationship selling	Wholesale price
Retail price	Consumer products
Cognitive dissonance	Vertical channels
Herizontal channels	Break even

The price which the store receives the product for.	The idea is to start a genuine relationship with the client, to listen to their needs and concerns, so that they will keep coming back.
Typically purchased in retail stores for personal or household use.	The price which the store sells the product for.
When all the levels of production and distribution for a product are owned by the same person.	When a person has second thoughts about whether they purchased the correct product.
Where total revenue equals total cost (fixed and variable expenses).	When companies on the same level of production team up.

NOTES

NOTES

NOTES

NOTES

NOTES